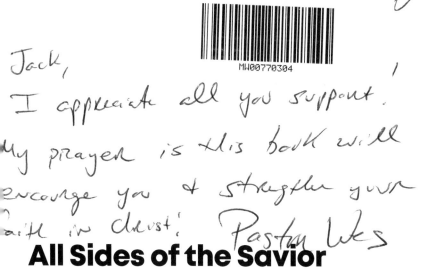

Jack,

I appreciate all you support.

My prayer is this book will

encourage you & strengthen your

faith in Christ! Pastor Wes

All Sides of the Savior

Exploring the Humanity of Jesus

Wes Feltner, Ph.D.

MW00770304

ISBN-13: 978-1-947153-15-8

Critical Mass Books

Layout by Rachel Greene

I will be forever grateful for all the support I received from home. Thank you for believing in me.

FOREWORD

In my two decades plus as a racetrack announcer all over the country, talk radio host in Minneapolis-St, Paul, and play-by-play broadcaster for the *Minnesota Vikings*, I have seen and endured a lot. I frequently give thanks to God for the wonderful professional existence he has provided me—and all of the unique people I have met. But all that is glittering might not always be gold.

Enter *All Sides of the Savior*.

When I heard Pastor Wes Feltner teach about *All Sides of the Savior*, I experienced the Word of God in a way I never had experienced before. I am 53 years old and have always had faith deeply rooted in my heart. *All Sides of the Savior* began as a series of weekly sessions carrying us through the humanity of Jesus Christ. It explained the human side of Jesus, *why* the humanity of Jesus is central to the gospel, and that God became human in order to redeem humanity.

All Sides of the Savior took for me what was a baseline life of faith and guided it to the next level. *All Sides of the Savior* shows how we can take The Word and human side of Jesus into our everyday lives and put it into practical use. For me, that involves kindness, being "Brutally Honest," "Righteously Angry," and being "Extravagantly Generous." These three examples are actual chapters in this book.

"Extravagantly Generous"—truly resonated with me because of my jobs and the thousands of people I can impact daily through my actions and the words I share. To give extravagantly does not have to be monetary, it can be better listening to those in need, always putting others before yourself, and better identifying those in need and, well, extravagant generosity.

Jesus doesn't just feed the crowd—he does so abundantly. Your appetite to learn and live the right way will be enhanced by your encounter with *All Sides of the Savior*.

If Jesus seems distant to you despite your faith, this book will make things more relatable. As the human side of Jesus comes alive, you will quickly realize that He was a human being like you and me.

Meeting Dr. Wes Felter and closely studying *All Sides of the Savior* has better helped me sow seeds of faith on a daily basis and handle adversity and daily struggles in my life. It has also helped me in sharing the importance of faith without becoming overbearing and turning off the listener.

Thanks to *All Sides of the Savior* and the heartfelt, comprehensive work done by Pastor Wes you are embarking on a journey of knowledge and faith into the human, relatable side of Jesus.

It's written in Matthew 11:28 that Jesus is "lowly in heart, and you will find rest for your souls." We all desire that and *All Sides of the Savior* will open your eyes and minds to edging closer to that reality.

Study. Absorb. Enjoy!

Paul Allen
The Voice of the Minnesota Vikings

CHAPTER ONE

Completely Human

How can you have a personal relationship with Jesus without knowing the full person of Jesus? That's the whole point of Christianity, isn't it—to have a personal relationship with Christ? But how is that possible if you only look at *half* of Him? How can you experience Jesus in your everyday life if you only see His deity and never see Jesus in His full humanity?

Remember Michael Jordan? He seemed almost supernatural when he played basketball. Surely no ordinary human could hang in the air for so long, or make basket after basket so effortlessly. He was referred to in the media as *Air Jordan*. Maybe you wish you could ask him for help with your game. But could he actually relate to your two left feet and inability to focus and follow through?

Not likely.

But Jordan wasn't born a champion. He had to work, and learn, and overcome. And when you begin to understand his strenuous efforts to *develop* those skills, it makes him more human—more approachable. You realize that you can do more than simply wonder at his ability—you can emulate it. And when you've failed again, or come up against something that seems too hard, you know he understands. His advice means so much more because he's been there.

In a much more profound way, having an accurate understanding of the *humanity* of Jesus will free you to relate to Him more honestly, to see yourself more realistically, and to experience an authentic relationship with Him. It all begins with the foundational truth that Jesus was, in fact, *completely human*.

Paul wrote about this to the church at Philippi. In theological terms, it's called the *kenosis*, which means "to empty." Jesus emptied Himself. Of what? Of His divine attributes. What does this mean? How did He do that? Paul explains.

> "Have this mind among yourselves, which is yours in Christ Jesus who, though He was in the form of God, did not count equality with God a thing to be grasped, **but emptied Himself** by taking the form of a servant, being born in the

likeness of men. Being found in human form, He humbled himself by becoming obedient to the point of death, even death on a cross."[1]

Let me ask you a question. Do you think Jesus ever got the stomach flu? I remember one day in seminary when one of my professors asked that question in class. Now, on a normal day, the overwhelming response of those in the class would have been, "Well, yeah, I mean, of course. It's possible. I mean, Jesus was human after all." But on that particular day, the response to that specific question was complicated. And the reason why it was complicated was because my professor was asking it right after a stomach virus had swept through the seminary community. The students in that room had literally just spent time hovering over a toilet, vomiting. They were still recovering from the weakness of that sickness. They were still tired from waking up in the middle of the night with cold sweats. It was in that critical moment of personal awareness that he posed the question, "Did Jesus ever get the stomach flu?"

In that moment, his question was anything but theoretical or incidental. It forced us to think about the humanity of Jesus, not in a generic way, but in a way that seemed undignified with regards to the King of Kings and Lord of Lords. Let me ask you, can you actually picture in your mind Jesus Christ on the side of the road bending

---

1. Philippians 2:5

over and puking His guts out because He had some bad fish? Not likely, because it's embarrassing. It feels somewhat disrespectful. In fact, it seems almost blasphemous. And yet, we need to look honestly at the human side of Jesus even if it makes us uncomfortable.

The reality is that we gladly testify that God became man to save us, but we don't want to think of God in terms of actually being a man. We readily affirm the humanity of Jesus, yet rarely think of Him as fully human. It goes against the way we've been conditioned to think about Jesus.

When you've only experienced something in a certain way, or only thought about something in a particular way, it's natural for that thing to seem strange when you're exposed to it in a different way. This happens all the time in life. You become so identified with a player for a specific team that it feels strange when you see that same player in the uniform of a different team. Maybe you've heard a word pronounced the exact same way all of your life, and then you hear it pronounced differently, and it seems strange. Pecan, for instance. Pe-CAN. PEE-can. Pe-CAHN. If you've seen or heard something the same way all your life and then it's presented differently, it can seem strange.

Could it be that we have so emphasized the divinity of Jesus (rightly so) that when we actually stop and think about His humanity, it feels strange? Even wrong?

Theologian Bruce Ware writes, "The instinct in much of evangelical theology, both popular and scholarly, is to stress the deity of Christ. But when it comes to the day-today obedience and ministry of Jesus, the New Testament puts greater stress on His humanity. He is the second Adam, the son of David. He lived His life as one of us. Now, again, He is fully and unequivocally God, but while He is fully God, the predominant reality He experienced day by day, which, in fact, fulfilled His calling, was His genuine and full humanity."[2]

Russ Moore writes, "Many of us see Jesus either as a ghostly friend in the corner of our hearts promising us heaven and guiding us through difficulty, or we see Him simply in terms of His sovereignty and power distant from us.... But bridging this distance is precisely at the heart of the gospel itself."[3]

The great truth of the ages is that the Word became *flesh*.[4] God became like us in order to save us. He lived a human life—just like yours. He was human—just like you!

But it's hard for us to have mental images of Jesus as feverish, vomiting, crying, and studying to learn Hebrew. In fact, from the beginning of the Christian era, there were those who sought to redefine the gospel, arguing that it doesn't seem right to think of Jesus as genuine flesh and bone filled with blood, intestines, and urine. However, Luke tells us that Jesus *grew* in wisdom and knowledge.

---

2. Bruce Ware *The Man Christ Jesus* (2012)
3. Russell Moore, T*he Humanity of Christ Matters* (blog 1/25/2012), https://www.russellmoore.com/2012/01/25/the-humanity-of-christ-matters/
4. John 1:14

He wasn't born with it. Yes, such things can seem to detract from His deity and dignity, but that's actually the point of the gospel. Becoming like Him flows from seeing Him as He *is.*[5]

The very beginning of the Christmas story tells us that the Messiah was wrapped in swaddling clothes. Why? For the same reason you diaper your baby. Don't you see? From the very beginning, Jesus was one of us, sharing the same human nervous system, human digestive system, and every aspect of human nature.

John Eldredge addressed this very thing when he wrote, "Crept in this notion has, and it's done great damage to our perceptions and experiences of Him. It's the notion that Jesus was really pretending when He presented Himself as man."

Will you worship Jesus Christ? Hold fast to the belief that He is God, "very God of very God," to be exact, as the Nicene Creed states. When we think of His heroic actions, His divine miraculous powers, we think of Him like Einstein dropping in on a first grade math quiz, or Mozart playing in a kindergarten choir. After all, we're talking about Jesus here, you know? The guy who walked on water, who raised Lazarus from the dead. He never broke a sweat. Right?

Now, you might think that keeping Jesus all mysterious and heavenly is proper, but consider this. When God inspired the writers of the Gospels to tell His story, Jesus was presented as a *man,* very much human, a

5. I John 3:2

person with a very distinct personality. We cannot deny the humanity of Jesus. And we must not merely accept it, but we must embrace the fullness of all that it means. God became a man. Do you realize that most of the early church heresies were over this issue? They just couldn't get their minds around the idea that God could actually become flesh.

Gnosticism, for instance. Gnostics, both then and now, view the physical world as evil and the spiritual as good, which was a very Platonic view of the world. So the idea that God would actually become flesh was repugnant. But so critical was this truth that the apostle John told the church, "By this you know the Spirit of God: every spirit that confesses that Jesus Christ has come *in the flesh* is from God, and every spirit that does not confess Jesus is not from God. This is the spirit of the antichrist, which you heard was coming and now is in the world already."[6] You must embrace and explore His humanity. You must see Him for who He is, fully God but also fully man. This foundational truth comes from scripture, not from my opinion. Not from other authors, but from the voice of God, which says that Jesus was completely human. Read that passage again: "*Have this mind among yourselves, which is yours in Christ Jesus who, though He was in the form of God, did not count equality with God a thing to be grasped, but emptied Himself by taking the form of a servant, being born in the likeness of men. Being found in human form, He humbled*

---

6. I John 4:2-3

Himself by becoming obedient to the point of death, even death on a cross."[7]

We start with the divinity of Jesus. No passage—other than the first chapter of John's gospel—shows more explicitly that Jesus is fully God. You'll notice the English phrase used repeatedly in Philippians: He was in the *form of God*, in the *form of a servant*, like man, and in *human form*. Now, on the surface, the word "form" might seem to refer to physical appearance only. Again, echoing early church heresies, someone coined the phrase that Jesus was just "God in a bod."

It's a good rhyme—God in a bod—but heretical in doctrine. This is where checking the translation is so important because there are two Greek words for "form." The first word is *morphe*, meaning the essence of something. The second word is *schema*, and it refers to the outer appearance or shape of something. Let me illustrate the difference between the two. When my daughter was born, her *morphe*, her essence was female, and she will always be female. Regardless of the cultural debate on gender, the reality is that she will always have two x chromosomes. Her essence is female. That's her *morphe*. But her *schema*, her outer form, changed significantly. She went from baby to toddler to a little girl in, like, two days.

At least it felt that way.

---

7. Philippians 2:5-8

In a short time, her outward shape changed a great deal, but her *morphe*, her essence has always been the same. One is essence, the other is outward shape. Paul used the Greek word *morphe* in his letter to the Philippians. That is, Jesus was the *essence* of God. He is God. He has the substance of God, the attributes of God. He is by very nature God. This isn't the only passage that testifies to this. "*In the beginning was the word, the word was with God, and the word was God.*"[8] He was there at the beginning with God. "*In Him* [Christ], *all the fullness of God was pleased to dwell.*"[9] In our current passage in Philippians, Paul said, "*He did not consider equality with God a thing to be grasped.*" To be taken advantage of. More about that later, but the point is that He had the attributes of God even though He set them aside.

Paul was clearly teaching the divinity of Jesus—that Jesus is fully God. Now, you might be thinking, "Wait a minute, I thought you set this whole thing up to be about the humanity of Jesus. Why are you talking so much about His divinity?" Well, for two reasons. First, I want to make it very clear that I am not denying His divinity and deity—that Jesus is God. And I didn't say "was" God. I'm saying *is* God. He *is* eternal God. The second reason that I'm emphasizing this is because once you feel the weight of Jesus being in the "form of God," you can then feel the weight of what Paul means when he says, "Jesus was in the form of man."

---

8. John 1:1
9. Colossians 1:19

"And being found in human form..."

This is exciting—and right on point. It's exactly the same word Paul used about Jesus being in the form of God. In other words, Jesus not only had the full essence of *divinity*, but He took on the full essence of *humanity*. You can't believe one and not believe the other. Jesus just didn't pretend to be a human. He really was human. The Bible clearly testifies to this fact. He became a human.

In fact, the Bible says He was conceived, He was born, He took on flesh and blood. The Bible not only says that He became a human, but He *lived* as a human. He was circumcised. He wept. He got hungry. He got thirsty. He slept. He got weary. He was grieved. He became angry. He needed to be alone at times. He felt the weight of temptation. This may make you uncomfortable, and that's okay, but Jesus was a *normal* guy.

You may be thinking, "heretic!" but hold on. You can't embrace His full divinity if you don't embrace His full humanity. He was human in every sense of that word. He didn't walk around in a white robe that miraculously never got dirty. He didn't walk around with a halo on His head like in some pictures. (It would have been pretty easy to figure out He was the Messiah. Just follow the guy with the halo.) That's not how Jesus is presented in the gospels at all. He had a mom and brothers—who didn't always agree with Him. He went to the temple, He asked questions, He had friends—some of whom betrayed Him. He celebrated holidays, spoke with a Galilean accent, got hungry, and He got tired.

He was a real man, a real human being. And He didn't just *become* a mature human being. He didn't just go through the motions of a human life. The Bible testifies to the fact that He *grew* as a human. The Bible says, for instance, that He increased in wisdom and stature, that He learned obedience through His suffering. That is, He didn't just become flesh, He continued becoming flesh in the same way that you and I do. His body changed and grew. He gained more information. He obtained more life experiences. As the author of Hebrew says, "*He was like us in every way.*"[10]

Think about that.

There are so many practical implications of the incarnation that I wish I could get into. But that would be another whole book. Perhaps several. There is so much significance for the Christian life in the incarnation. You see, there's an unfortunate dichotomy that people often have in their view of Christianity: they either think the Christian life is spiritual—you study, pray, talk to people about Jesus, sing songs to get a spiritual feeling—or it's just all physical—you go to church, care for the poor, do good works, and present your bodies as sacrifices of worship.

But the incarnation says, "It's not this or that, it's this *and* that." It's both. It's not just me and my quiet time with Jesus, it's actually caring for my body and serving with my hands and presenting my physical life as worship to God.

---

10. Hebrews 2:17

It's spiritual *and* physical.

Some believe what really matters is the spirit inside, and that the body is not a part of our personhood. You hear this sometimes even at funerals. I've heard people say, "Well, don't worry about your loved one...this is just her shell. What really matters is that her spirit is in Heaven." Nonsense. While I'm not denying the comfort in "to be absent from the body is to be present with the Lord," let's be clear. The body is vital a part of our personhood. Our humanity. Her body was created in the image of God. Separating spirit and soul and body is not a good thing. We are holistic beings. In fact, when God became a man, do you know what He was telling us?

Matter *matters*.

The physical creation of God is a good thing. At the end of each day during creation, God said, "It is good." Creation may be broken by sin, but it was good enough that God willingly came into it. This reality has implications for gender and marriage—biology actually matters. It's not what you feel on the inside or what your spiritual person is. No, you are a whole being. God became man and that matters.

The fact that God took on a human life also means your life matters to God. God came into our world and took on our life. Do you realize how significant your life is to Him? It's not that I'm making you the center of things. I'm simply saying God actually cares. Because if He didn't actually care, why would He ever take on flesh? But He so loves human beings that He became one. It means the highs and the lows of your life, birth and death, gorgeous sunrises and sunsets, love, beauty, relationships, work, a good drink, beautiful music, and a nice meal—all of the things that make up this life are a part of God's good creation. Let us not forget that in the beginning when God finished with all of His creation, He declared it all to be very good! It matters to Him because it's you.

That's good news.

The fact that Jesus is God *and* man is at the heart of the good news of the gospel. You might ask, "How do these things work together?" He's fully divine. The Bible clearly teaches that. He's fully human. The Bible clearly teaches that. But when Jesus was on Earth, how did it work? Look at what Paul said to the Philippians, *"Though He was in the form of God, He did not count equality with God a thing to be grasped, but He emptied himself by taking the form of a servant being born in the likeness of men."*[11]

This crystallized what the early Christians believed about Jesus and what Jesus taught about Himself. Namely, that He had all the divine attributes. He didn't get rid of them, but *He did not take advantage of them or use them to His gain* as He was living life on Earth. Which is why Paul was using Jesus as the ultimate example of not taking advantage of His rights in order to serve others. That's what Paul meant by "He emptied himself." Notice the wording. Jesus did not pour something out of Himself, He poured Himself out. That's huge. He kept His divinity.

---

11. Philippians 2:6-7, ESV

He didn't give up His divinity. He gave up His *rights*. He still had divine essence and attributes and abilities, but He didn't use them. Why?

He wanted to live the life of a servant.

Illustrations or metaphors about this are difficult, because this truth is so profound. But here is a very simple and inadequate one that will still give a mental picture. When my kids were little, we loved to wrestle. I would get down and wrestle with them on the ground. Yet, while on the ground wrestling with my kids, I still had all of my attributes. I was still dad. I still had my "lightning quick" reflexes, I had my "Herculean" muscles. I had all the attributes that made me who I am. But in those moments, I didn't use them. It's not a perfect illustration, but it gives a picture of how Jesus still had all those attributes, but didn't use them. He emptied himself so that He could be a servant in the form, the *morphe*, of humanity.

Here's another example from Bruce Ware. "Imagine a king who rules the kingdom. And he has everything: servants, wardrobe, all the food that he could possibly want. One day the king observes beggars in the street. He has compassion on them and wants to help them. The king decides that in order to help them, he needs to become like them. While still remaining King and retaining all his rights, authority, and riches, he takes off his royal garments and puts on the clothes of a beggar."[12]

---

12. Bruce Ware "The Man Christ Jesus," page 22

He lived exactly as they lived, begging for food and sleeping on the cold streets. People passed by and mocked and spat. The king suffered. He wasn't faking it. He genuinely experienced that life, and he really suffered. As king, he could have called for his army at any time, but he chose not to because he couldn't do that and fully experience life as a beggar.

Now, listen to that last statement. To fully experience the beggar's life, he laid aside not his kingship, but his *rights* as king. That is what Paul was getting at. Jesus is fully divine, and He is fully human, but He did not use or take advantage of His divine attributes as He was living on earth. This means that most of the time in the gospels, what you think is Jesus showing that He's God is actually Jesus showing that He's human. You may wonder, "What does that mean?" Let me give two examples.

First, His miracles. Here's an example from Matthew. "*And He went throughout Galilee teaching in their synagogues and proclaiming the gospel of the kingdom and healing every disease, every affliction among the people.*"[13] His fame had spread throughout all Syria. They brought in the sick, afflicted with various diseases and pains, those oppressed by demons, those having seizures, and paralytics and He healed them. Stop. I guarantee that most Christians reading that passage think, "Well, that's Jesus showing that He's God. 'Watch all my miracles as I show you that I am actually God.'" Wrong. Not that He's not actually God, of course. He is. But remember what

---

13. Matthew 4:23

Paul said to the Philippians—He set those things aside. He's not showing you that He's God. He's showing you that He's really human. How, so? Go back to the very beginning of scripture. Do you remember the first two human beings? What were they given? They were given dominion and authority over creation.

What Jesus was showing us in Matthew's account was not "Look at me, I'm God." Jesus was saying, "Look at me, I am the real human Messiah, I am the one promised long ago, I am the ultimate Adam, and I am the one who can make right everything sin made wrong." He wasn't telling you to look at divinity. He was telling you to look at humanity. "You were created to rule the world. Sin tore that apart, but the ultimate human in the image of God is now here. Follow me and I'll take you back there." This is why, when John the Baptist asked for a sign that Jesus was the true Messiah (anointed human), Jesus said, "The lame walk and the dead are raised." His miracles demonstrated dominion over creation. He was the true human. The true Adam.

The second example has to do with His knowledge. Do you remember the conversation with the Samaritan woman at the well?[14] Jesus said to her, "Go call your husband and come here." The woman said, "I have no husband." Jesus replied, "You're right in saying 'I have no husband,' for

---

14. John 4:16, ESV

you have five. And the one you now have is not your husband, what you have said is true."

I guarantee most read that and think, "Well, there's Jesus showing that He's God. He's showing the attribute of omniscience, that He knows all." But that is not what Jesus was showing, even though He had the attribute of omniscience. Remember, it says in Philippians chapter two that Jesus didn't use His divine attributes to His advantage. You may ask, "Then what was He doing?"

He was using His prophetic discernment just like the Old Testament prophets did.

Need proof? Look at her response, "Sir, I perceive that you are a prophet." Jesus was showing her that He was the Messiah, the *human being* who had the spirit of God and spoke truth.

Those are just two examples of how we often ascribe Jesus' actions to His divinity—something that isn't accessible to *us,* so we disregard the action as irrelevant to us personally. He was still divine. In that moment, He was every bit God, but that wasn't what He was showing us.

He was displaying true *humanity.*

Why does this matter? Why do we need to understand the person of Jesus in His full humanity? First, until we see all sides of the Savior, we'll never worship Jesus for who He really is. We shouldn't have a one-dimensional view of Jesus. We need to understand more about Jesus than just His compassion or righteousness so that we can worship fully.

Next, until we see all sides of the Savior, we will never understand what it really means *to us* to be human. A woman came up to me after a church service not long ago and said, "I'm 64 years old. I've never thought of this before." Most of us make assumptions about what it means to be human based on fallen humanity, not true humanity. We excuse our bitterness, rage, lust, and envy by saying things like, "Well, I'm only human." The truth is, when we look at the humanity of Jesus, we see that those things aren't human at all. They're actually more devilish than human.

Do you really want to know what it's like to be human? Do you really want to understand all that it means to be *humane*? Then don't look around you to fallen humanity, look to the perfect example of true humanity. His name is Jesus Christ. I want you to understand what it really means to be you. And the only way you'll ever do that is to understand more of Him. Only then will you begin to understand what your life was meant to be.

Finally, until we see all sides of this Savior, we will never fully experience Jesus in the everyday life. As you gain a deeper understanding that Jesus knows what it's like to have a prayer rejected, to have friends betray Him, to feel lonely, to face death, to lose a loved one, to laugh and love, to weep and be angry. Only when you understand this will you rush to Him first in every circumstance.

Part of the reason we don't run to Him in daily life is because we don't believe He's actually lived this life. But if we've really begun to see Jesus in all of His humanity and we lose a loved one, where else would we run but to the one who knows exactly what that's like because He *has,* in every way, lived our life. Soon, we will discover Jesus there with us in laughter and in love and in sorrow and in grief, and realize that He has always been there.

I don't know if Jesus ever got a stomach bug. It's possible. The Bible doesn't say. But I know this, if you think that it is undignified to think of Jesus in that way, may I remind you that Jesus experienced something far more undignified and embarrassing than that.

If you can't picture Jesus waking up in the night in a cold sweat, how are you ever going to see Him in the night sweating drops of blood? If you can't picture Jesus asking for something to drink to ease His sick stomach, how will you ever see Him saying "I thirst," as He hung on a cross? If you can't see Jesus waking up the next day, sun piercing through the window, knowing the sickness He fought all night is gone, how will you see Him as the one who woke up one morning, sun piercing through the stone as He walked out of that grave? Until we understand the person of Jesus, we will not understand what Paul meant when He said these words, "*There is one God, and there is one mediator between God and men,* **the man**, *Christ Jesus.*"[15]

---

15. 1 Timothy 2:5

CHAPTER TWO

Righteously Angry

"The Passover of the Jews was at hand and Jesus went up to Jerusalem. In the temple, he found those who were selling oxen and sheep and pigeons, and the money changers sitting there. Making a whip of cords, he drove them all out of the temple. With the sheep and oxen, he poured out the coins of the money changers and overturned their tables. He told those who sold the pigeons, 'Take these things away, do not make my Father's house a house of trade.' His disciples remembered that it was written, 'Zeal for your house will consume me.' So the Jews

said to him, 'What sign do you show us for doing these things?' And Jesus answered them, 'Destroy this temple. And in three days, I will raise it up.' The Jews then said, 'It's taken 46 years to build this temple and you raise it up in three days?' But he was speaking about the temple of his body. When therefore he was raised from the dead, his disciples remembered that he had said this and they believed the Scripture and the word that Jesus had spoken."[16]

As he got closer to the city, his excitement grew. It didn't matter that he had traveled more than 850 miles on foot, or that his small travel fund made him sleep in uncomfortable places. It didn't even matter that he got ill along the way—so sick he almost died. None of that mattered now. It was all behind him as he stood at the edge of the city. He was so filled with joy that he literally knelt down and kissed the ground. He couldn't wait to visit the sacred sites, look at the shrines, and interact with the priests. He knew that it was going to be an experience he would never forget. But, much to his disappointment, he would soon realize that Rome was not anything like he thought it would be.

It was October in the year 1510 when Martin Luther was sent to Rome. He thought it was going to be a place full of piety, godliness, ministry, and worship. But that

---

16 John 2:12-22, ESV

was not what he experienced. Luther did not find Rome to be a place of spirituality and splendor, but rather a place of sanctimony and sewage. It was not a place where one could stop and pray, but rather, a place where impatient priests hurried him along. It was a place where he thought the clergy would be serving people, instead he found them taking advantage of the poor, selling things called indulgences, with which, for a fee, one could free a family member from purgatory. The religious leaders said things like, "Don't you hear your family members screaming in anguish? You realize that you could free them for just a little bit of money?" They even convinced Luther to try to free his own grandfather, but his doubts grew with every step as he climbed toward the high doors of the cathedral.

He wasn't doubting God—he was doubting Rome.

He stood at the top of the steps looking out over what he now saw as a circus—and a man once full of anticipation was now filled with anger. Why? Because what he saw wasn't right. He saw immorality, injustice, poverty, greed, and manipulation. It bothered him at his very core.

Have you ever looked out on the world the way Luther looked out on Rome and been bothered by what you saw? Has that ever happened to you? Has observing a fallen world ever made your temperature rise? Have you felt like the Apostle Paul who looked around Athens—a place full of idolatry—and become deeply troubled?[17]

---

17 Acts 17:16

My guess is that you have experienced this before. Maybe you get angry when you see the elderly taken advantage of. Maybe you get angry when you see children who are abused. Maybe you get angry when you see human life treated with very little value. Maybe you get angry when you watch a disease destroy a mind and body. Maybe you get angry when you watch death take another life. The reality is that sometimes life in a *fallen* world will make your temperature *rise*. You may say, "Oh, no, no, not me. I'm always happy. I don't ever get angry. The only emoji on my cellphone is the happy face."

But I suggest to you that there are things in this life to which the only *proper* response is righteous anger. Now, that word "righteous" is very important. I'm not just talking about anger for anger's sake. I'm talking about a rightly focused anger. I'm not talking about petty things like parking spots or the volume of music in church. And I'm not suggesting that anyone should ever act, speak, or behave in a way that dishonors Christ. Absolutely not. I'm simply saying there are things in this present fallen world that should make your temperature rise. That's exactly the side of the Savior John described in chapter two. It was almost time for the Jewish Passover, and Jesus went up to Jerusalem. He went into the big, open court of the temple and found people selling oxen, sheep, and doves, and the money changers were sitting there.

Before we dive into the details of the story, I want to deal with a common question. Sometimes people will suggest that this passage represents "a contradiction in the Bible." The reason they say this is because in John's

Gospel, this episode is placed at the beginning of Jesus' ministry. And in Matthew, Mark and Luke, it's placed at the end of Jesus' ministry. But it's not actually a contradiction. There are possibly two things happening. First, the incidence could have happened more than once. Some scholars believe that this happened at the beginning of His ministry and again at the end.

More likely, however, those who call this a contradiction are operating under an incorrect assumption that the Gospel authors were relating a *chronology*. They were not. Though they often related stories of actual, literal events in the order they happened (e.g., in the *Synoptic* Gospels—Matthew, Mark, and Luke), their purpose was not to write a biography or to document mere history, it was to introduce the Savior. So, they wrote topically from their own viewpoints.

Whether John was taking one event and bringing it to the front for topical reasons or whether it was something that happened twice, in no way is there a contradiction in scripture. Whichever episode you take in the four accounts, it was at Passover, the annual celebration of Israel's rescue from Egypt. Jerusalem was swarming with people. There were thousands of pilgrims from all around the Roman Empire. Hotels were booked. Homes were filled with out-of-town guests. There were tents surrounding the city where people stayed. In fact, it's estimated that two and one quarter million Jewish males had traveled to Jerusalem for the Passover.

Wall-to-wall people.

The focus of everything was the massive temple. It was the center of everything, the focus of everyone's attention. All the visitors wanted their picture made by it. They wanted to send a postcard of it back to their family. They wanted to get a little Temple snow globe at the souvenir shop. And being Jewish, they had to offer a sacrifice. Well, as you know, even today wherever the crowds go, so does commerce. People had begun to take advantage of this opportunity. As a man entered the temple court, the first thing he would encounter was the money changers.

The temple had its own *currency*.

To operate in the temple, he needed that currency. So, if he was from out-of-town and had a different kind of currency, he had to exchange it. Needless to say, the exchange rate was not in his favor, but he had to do it. Once the money had been exchanged, he'd go a little farther. He had to have an animal sacrifice, so some enterprising people set up shop there to make it convenient for a true worshipper to buy one on the spot. One might ask, "Well, what if he brought his own sacrifice?" BYOS. Well, it didn't really work that way because if he had traveled from a great distance, he couldn't bring a sacrifice that distance because it had to be without blemish and it wouldn't be presentable any longer. And even if he did, or he bought one on the way, it had to pass the Ancient Near Eastern version of TSA.

They would inspect whatever sacrifice was presented, critically, and from every angle. And if there was any spot, any blemish, they would not allow it. He'd have to buy one from the Temple. Now, they might not tell him they'd keep his and sell it to the next guy, but, as is typical at any professional sporting event today, what cost $5 on the streets was $75 inside the temple. As you might imagine, people were often frustrated with what was going on. Robbery, complaining, theft, people being taken advantage of, all of it was happening in a place of *worship*.

Imagine you show up at church on a Sunday morning and there's a line to get into the parking lot. They make you pay $20 for parking. Except they don't take US currency. You need to have their particular church currency bearing the church's logo. It's the only money that will be accepted. By the time you've exchanged your dollars for the coins, you've actually paid $35 to park.

Then, when you get out of your car and try to enter the church building, they make you buy a ticket. And there is a mandatory two-coffee minimum. You can't bring in your *Caribou* or *Starbucks*. Nope. It has to be the church brand, holier, more sanctified coffee. One might even say, Holy *Grounds*. That costs you another twenty bucks. By now, you're fairly frustrated. You kind of want to leave, but the law requires you to be here, and the police are parked right outside. Do the math. You decide you're going to find your seat, but you realize you can't sit wherever you want to.

Of course you can't.

If you're a Southerner, your seating section is out in the commons. Norwegian women, well, you are up in the balcony (but Norwegian *men* can sit a little closer). If you are on the staff at the church, you get the front-row theater seats. If you are on the *Pastoral* Staff, well then, you get back-stage access, where there's a hot tub and fine Cuban *Cohibas*. By the time you get done with your Sunday morning experience, you have heard so much whispering, gossiping, and manipulation—and been cheated out of so much money—that you feel like you've been to something more resembling a circus than a church. That's what Jesus walked into. It was the temple. The place where God met with man.

And this was what it had become?

Now look at the side of the Savior that came out. *"And making a whip of cords. He drove them all out of the temple with the sheep and oxen. He poured out the coins of the money changers and overturned their tables. He told those who sold pigeons, 'Take these things away. Do not make my Father's house a house of trade.'"*

Jesus got angry. As we say in the South, he got His knickers in a knot. He was really, really mad. This is not the side of the Savior that we often think about. We tend to think of Jesus as meek and mild, not angry. As I researched this incident, I was shocked by how many people I came across in my reading and study who actually tried to downplay this. They said things like, "Oh, Jesus wasn't really angry. He was just trying to get people's attention."

Nonsense.

He made a whip. It didn't say He brought a whip. It didn't say He had a whip. It said He intentionally sought out the components to make a whip, and He didn't stop there. He turned over the tables. The text says He drove all of the merchants and their animals out. The temple courts, several hundred yards of area, were full of people. The likely section where the moneylenders and vendors were was roughly the size of a football field. There had to have been a large number of merchants and many animals in pens. It would have been very much like a stockyard in that area. And Jesus ran them all out—their sheep and oxen with them. Then He looked the dove sellers in the eye and He said, "Get this stuff out of here. Stop turning my Father's house into a market!" Jesus was angry—righteously! Now, what does this side of our Savior teach us?

Two things Jesus is *not*, and one thing Jesus *is*.

First of all, it's very clear that Jesus was not a *pacifist*. People often try to portray Jesus like a hippie, just about peace, love, and unity. As though He walked around talking like a dope-head. "Hi, how ya doin'? Hey, don't make my Father's house a place of trade, okay? I'm serious. Stop it. I mean it. Don't make me mad, okay?"

He's presented as boring and stale, like He spent His whole day rescuing kittens out of sycamore trees, and as though the essence of His ministry was just to make everyone feel good. Wrong. He was passionate. He rebuked. He said that He divided families. The point is, a passive Jesus is not the Jesus of Scripture. Don't explain away this side of Jesus or you won't have the real one. He was and is not passive.

Second, we need to also understand that He didn't have a short fuse. He wasn't acting like the *Incredible Hulk* where one minute everything's normal and the next minute He was going *off* on people. He didn't have a bad day, or get up on the wrong side of the bed, and just decide to throw a *temple tantrum*. It's not that Jesus was having a bad day like we sometimes do, and just lost it. There was something else going on. Why did He respond in this way? What was going on? Let's let John tell us.

"*His disciples remembered that it was written, zeal for your house will consume me.*"[18] This is a reference from the Psalms.[19] Literally, that phrase means to eat you up. "Zeal for your house," that is, for God's house, "will consume me." That is what was happening in Jesus. That is what brought out this side of the Savior. He was zealous. The human Jesus was passionate for the things of God. I want to take it one step further, because revealed in this righteous anger of Jesus is a real love for us.

Jesus cares passionately about us having a relationship with God. It was and is His whole mission. The reason why He came was so that man and God could be reconciled. So when He saw the Temple, the place that had been set aside for connection with God, to focus on God, being used by a bunch of corrupt men with misplaced priorities, placing barriers between His people and God, He got righteously angry.

---

18 John 2:17
19 Psalm 69:9

There is nothing more important in all of life than your communion with God. So if Jesus sees things in your life that are hindering that, because He loves you so much, He will not hesitate to come in and righteously turn the tables in your heart upside down.

Consider what Jesus was doing that day and why He responded that way. What lessons are there for us to learn today? I wonder what Jesus would say if He walked into my church, into my heart. If He walked into your heart, what would He see? I want to give you four things to really think about in terms of what makes Jesus righteously angry in our lives and in our worship. The four things are to different categories of people: Christian leaders, Christian churches, Christians in general, and then to everybody.

To Christian Leaders
Jesus gets righteously angry when desire for gain replaces desire for God

Jesus cannot stand it when Christian leaders, like leaders there in the Temple, focus on their profit instead of God's praise. They were supposed to be celebrating the Passover, not cashing in on it. Christian leaders, do you realize what *your* calling is about? Do you realize what ministry is ultimately about? It's not about building your platform.

It's not about building your wallet. It's not about making a name for yourself. It's about helping people connect with God. When you turn it into something else, Jesus gets righteously angry.

That's a word to me—and all pastors. That's a word to Christian leaders everywhere. When you make ministry about profit, rather than connecting people with God, Jesus wants to turn your tables over. Let me show you how He did it with the Pharisees. He said, "Woe to you scribes and Pharisees, hypocrites, for you clean the outside of the cup and the plate, but inside you're full of greed and self-indulgence."[20]

Jesus cannot stand it when Christian leaders, specifically, mask their greed with a form of godliness. There are many examples of which I will not name names, but some may come to mind as you read this. The ministry is about serving people that they might be connected with God.

To Christian Churches
Jesus gets righteously angry when ministry is primarily for those on the inside

Jesus gets fired up when ministry inside—because this was happening inside of the temple grounds—is really *only* for those on the inside. In another gospel account of this story, Jesus used this phrase when He said, "My house

---

20 Matthew 23:25

will be called a house of prayer for all nations, but you have turned it into a den of robbers."[21] Now, don't think that the point is just prayer. It's actually bigger than that because Jesus is quoting from Isaiah where God says, "...for my house will be called a house of prayer for all nations."[22]

The Jewish Temple had an area that was called the Gentile Court. It may have been where the merchants and moneychangers had set up shop. The Gentile Court was where those who were non-Jews, outsiders, anybody from anywhere could come in and pray. All were welcome to enter in there. The problem was that the religious leaders had become so consumed with commerce and making a profit that they had "expanded their ministries." They were offering a service, after all, and had pushed into the Gentile Court and now the outsiders couldn't come in.

You may ask, "Well, what does that have to do with us as the church?" Nothing gets Jesus angrier than when the church becomes so focused on the ministry inside that they forget the Great Commission. We must remember that we don't exist to be a holy huddle, a little fellowship of insiders so comfortable in our little groups that we actually become a hindrance to outsiders who are trying to come in and understand how they can have a relationship with God. Our mission is to make disciples of all nations, not to play church until we go be with Jesus.

---

21 Mark 11:17
22 Isaiah 56:7

When ministry inside becomes only for those on the inside, Jesus wants to turn the tables over.

To Christian People
Jesus gets righteously angry when the motions of worship replace the meaning of worship

The temple was full of activity. There were so many people. There were lots of programs. There was a lot of sacrifice going on, but Jesus saw past all of that. There was a lot of commotion and religious activity happening, but Jesus knew what was actually going on in the heart. *"Now while he was in Jerusalem at the Passover Festival, many believed in his name when they saw the signs that he was doing, but Jesus did not entrust himself to them because he knew all people. And he needed no one to bear witness about man for he himself knew what was in man."*[23]

Jesus can look right through all of our religious activity. This is what He came to do. Jesus didn't die on the cross so that we could have a nice religious routine on Sunday morning. He died on the cross and rose from the grave so that we could have a relationship with God. Jesus wants to turn our tables over because He came and died not so that we could enter into a church, but into the presence of God.

This reminds me of a story I read one time about a businessman on a flight. He received his in-flight meal

---

23 John 2:23

and when he opened it there was a roach inside. Obviously, he was infuriated by this. He wrote a letter to the airline expressing his anger. They responded, shockingly, with a very gracious letter: *"We are so sorry for this. It'll never happen again. We've cleaned the plane from top to bottom. Trust me. This will never happen again. Continue to fly with us."*

And he was encouraged by the letter until he saw something on the back; a little sticky note. So he flipped it over and read, *"Send this man the standard roach letter."* Now, think about that. The letter sounded good. It used all the right words. For a moment, the businessman even felt like it was sincere. But the truth was that it was nothing more than a routine action filled with meaningless words. We must not let that ever describe our worship. Jesus definitely wants to turn the tables over when He sees you going through the motions. Why?

Because He wants more for you.

To Everybody
Jesus gets righteously angry when symbols overshadow the Savior

Notice the dialogue that took place after Jesus had driven out all of the merchants and their livestock. Jesus said something that got right to the heart of the issue. The Jews said to him, *"What sign can you show us to prove your authority to do these things?"* Jesus answered them, *"Destroy this temple, and in three days I'll raise it up. They* replied, 'What? It's taken forty-six years to build this temple. You're going to raise it up in three days?" But the temple he had spoken of was his body."[24]

You see, Jesus had come to *replace* the temple. The symbol that had existed for all those years was always pointing to a Savior. Here's what Jesus was saying, and it is very important for us to understand: *Sometimes you can miss the Temple for the temple.*

You can become so fixated on symbols, so absorbed in the forms, that you miss that those things are actually pointing you to a *person*. You may wear a cross around your neck, carry a Bible, regularly attend a church, have a fish on your car, and a Scripture verse on your business card—you may have all the symbols, and still not have the Savior.

What an awful thing it would be to miss the Savior for all the symbols. To have all of the trappings of Christianity substituting for the actual person, Christ Jesus. That's what Jesus was teaching.

"*Don't you understand? I have come to replace the temple. I'm not talking about the temple that was built in forty-six years. I'm talking about the Temple that they crucified on a cross and three days later walked out of the grave.*" And because of that Temple that was the person of Jesus Christ, you can have a relationship with God. Do you have that relationship?

Don't miss the Savior for all the symbols.

---

24 John 2:18

So, if Jesus walked into the temple of your heart, what would He see? Would He see a desire for gain or a desire for God? Would He see a focus on self or would He see a focus on others? Would He see you just going through religious motions, or would He see somebody who really wants to worship God? Would He see someone who has all the substitutes, but has yet to find a Savior? May Jesus, by His grace, turn our tables over so that we might truly know God.

In the final scene of C.S. Lewis's *Voyage of the Dawn Treader,* Lucy and her friends are sailing on the farthest eastern sea. As they approach the final landing, they notice a large grassy area with a white spot. When they get closer, they realize that the white spot is actually a lamb cooking a meal on the shore. They wade to the beach, and they eat with this lamb. They enjoy fellowship with this lamb. They begin asking questions about the Land of Aslan, the great lion. And while they are asking, something amazing starts to happen to the lamb. Here's how Lewis records it. He says, "His snowy white flushed to gold and his size changed. It was Aslan himself towering above them and scattering the light with his mane." This was Lewis's way of showing what the Bible teaches us.

Jesus is not just a lamb. Jesus is a lion. He is not just gentle and meek, He is passionate. And you know what He's passionate about? He's passionate that you would know God.

CHAPTER THREE

Unquestionably Alive

"Now when Jesus came, they found that Lazarus had already been in the tomb four days. Bethany was near Jerusalem, about two miles off, and many of the Jews would come to Martha and Mary to console them concerning their brother. So when Martha heard that Jesus was coming, she went and met him, but Mary remained seated in the house.' Martha said to Jesus Lord, 'If you had been here, my brother would not have died. But even now I know that whatever you ask from God, God will give you. Jesus said to her, 'Your brother will rise again.' Martha said to him,

'I know that he will rise again in the resurrection on the last day.' Jesus said to her, 'I am the resurrection and the life. Whoever believes in me, though he dies, yet he shall live. And everyone who lives and believes in me shall never die. Do you believe this?' And she said to him, 'Yes, Lord. I believe that you are the Christ, the Son of God, who is coming into the world.'"[25]

"What do you think?
It's a match. You agree?
I agree. You have made me a happy man. Let's drink to it. To you!
No, to you!
To our agreement, to our prosperity, to our health and happiness. And most important of all, to life. L'Chaim.
L'Chaim, to life."

You may have recognized this exchange from the popular Broadway musical *Fiddler on the Roof.* That word—L'Chaim—is actually central to Jewish culture. The word comes from a Hebrew root word, which means, 'to be *alive.*' This mindset has always been a central part of a Judaic worldview. Life is something very precious and to be respected. It goes all the way back to Moses.

---

25 John 11:17-27

For instance, in the Book of Deuteronomy, Moses says this: "*Therefore choose life, that you and your offspring may live, loving the Lord your God, obeying his voice and holding fast to him, for **he is your life** and length of days.*"[26]

In other words, L'Chaim, to life.

Even if you do not consider yourself a religious person, you likely still resonate with that concept because all human beings know, deep down, that there is something wonderful and beautiful and precious about life.

We feel it when holding a newborn baby. When we watch a sunrise on a new day. That feeling of falling in love. A flower as it begins to bloom. The enjoyment of a really good meal. Laughter with a friend, and, of course, grandchildren.

Especially, grandchildren.

But we also know that feeling on the other side of the emotional spectrum—the grieving of life when it's gone. Though we may express it differently, all of us, in some way, have a toast of L'Chaim, to life.

This past Easter, as I was preparing to preach, it occurred to me that often we approach the Easter message from the angle of death. We've been a little too one-sided. If you listen to ten Easter messages, most of them will put the accent on death.

We tend to ask questions like, "Where will you spend eternity after you die?" Or, "Do you have hope in death?"

---

26 Deuteronomy 30:19-20

Inevitably, the *Captain Obvious* question is asked, "Did you know that you are going to die?" And you're sitting there thinking, "Yeah, I knew that. Thanks for reminding me. Way to be a downer."

I'm not suggesting that those questions are not appropriate. They're very appropriate. I have asked them all before. All I'm suggesting is that it can be a bit one-sided.

The resurrection of Christ doesn't only give us hope for inevitable death to come someday, it gives us hope to *live* today—L'Chaim. This reminds me of one of my favorite lines from an old TV western called *Lonesome Dove*, with Robert Duvall and Tommy Lee Jones. These two guys are Texas Rangers. They're best friends, but couldn't be more opposite. Woodrow is stern, and serious, and focused. Gus is a party looking for a place to happen. They've got this mutual friend who's in trouble, and they're talking about going to help her. Gus wants to help her out but Woodrow doesn't want to get involved. Woodrow looks at Gus in a very heated exchange and says, "Gus, if you go up there, you'll end up dying." And Gus looks back at Woodrow and says, "You just don't get it, do you? It ain't dying I'm talking about. It's living."

It is important for us to understand that the good news of the resurrection of Jesus Christ isn't about dying. It's about living. Real living. Abundant living. Living the kind of life that God created humans to live. And that is exactly what we see in this portion of the Gospel of John.

We are introduced to a man by the name of Lazarus. He is on his death bed. Hospice has left. The family has been called in. The sisters, Mary and Martha, realize the urgency of the situation, and so they call out for their dear friend, Jesus. They know His power. They've seen His miracles.

They know that nothing is impossible with this man.

Everyone, religious or not, looks to someone or something to provide peace in times of crisis. Everyone has faith in *something*, the question is do you have faith in the right thing? Even if you say, "I'm not a person of faith," the reality is yes, you are. You put faith in something. It may be yourself, it may be your family, it may be your good works, it may be the government, even, but everybody looks to something. Mary and Martha cried out for Jesus to come and help. A day passes, but Jesus still hasn't shown. Now, what could be taking Him so long? Maybe there's been a blizzard. Maybe Jesus' Uber broke down along the way. But whatever the reason, I'm sure it's a good one.

So, where *was* Jesus? John says that when Jesus heard that Lazarus was ill, He stayed two days longer where He was. That's not the kind of response you would expect to get from a guy who has built his ministry on helping people in need. His compassion was already legendary, and John tells us that Jesus *loved* Lazarus as a personal friend. What was going on?

Then it got worse.

"*Then Jesus told them plainly, 'Lazarus has died, and for your sake, I am glad that I was not there.'*" Are you serious? Jesus just said *that*? He is not only a no-show—he brags about it. Imagine that you have a loved one, someone you care deeply about. They've been rushed to the ER, and it's life-threatening. You call out for a pastor, but that pastor ignores your call and, let's say, continues fishing. Then he has the audacity to show up at the funeral a few days later and say, "I am so glad I wasn't there for you." You'd be upset. Probably angry. Definitely hurt. Why did Jesus do this? Why did He respond this way? It doesn't seem to reconcile with what we think about Jesus.

The truth is that, geographically, Jesus was far enough away that, even if He had left immediately, He wouldn't have been there before Lazarus died anyway. So He waited two days to make sure that there was no doubt at all. Lazarus was definitely dead.

Now, here's the important point: Jesus had a plan. We'll see that as the text unfolds. He always has a plan. You may say, "Well, I don't like His plan." That's okay. J. Vernon McGhee put it this way: "This is God's universe. He does things His way. You may have a better way, but you don't have a universe."[27] That's just how it works. You may think you have a better plan, but it's His universe. And He always has a plan.

---

27 *Thru the Bible commentary series: Ephesians,* p. 76, Dr. J. Vernon McGee

Look at the different ways that people responded to this seeming carelessness of Jesus. If we're honest, I think we can all find ourselves in their responses. John wrote, "When Martha heard that Jesus was coming, she went and met him. But Mary remained seated in the house."[28] One response was *distancing*. Mary didn't go out to meet him.

When we don't understand or have confidence in God's plan, we can become very distant in our relationship with God. Mary, Martha, and Lazarus were close personal friends of Jesus. This was a significant relationship for them, and Mary was hurt when He didn't run to help them. She was devastated by what felt like rejection—dismissal.

Remember, she was the one who sat at His feet drinking in His words when He came to visit. I can imagine her sitting in that dark house thinking, "I thought we mattered to Him. I thought He cared. I thought He was as committed to us as we were to Him. But He wasn't here when we needed Him most. I can't count on Him. I can't let Him hurt me like this again." Have you ever had thoughts like that when you were in pain or trouble?

I have.

This was a turning point for Mary. This event was when it all changed for her. Before Lazarus died, Mary was a friend and a starry-eyed fan of Jesus. But after this event, in the last week before He was crucified, we see a deeply committed, mature follower, recognizing His purpose

---

28 John 11:20

while other disciples were still denying that He could ever *die.* When she anointed Him for His death, pouring precious oil on his feet and wiping them with her hair in an act of deeply personal devotion, Jesus, Himself, said that she did it for His burial. Her first instinct may have been to distance herself from Him.

But Jesus had a plan for Mary.

Then there was Martha's response. Martha said to Jesus, "Lord, if you had been here, my brother would not have died." Does this voice of disappointment sound familiar to you? "Jesus, where were You? Why didn't You show up on time? Why didn't You come through when I really needed You?" Have you ever been disappointed with God?

I've been *there,* too.

It's like my calendar and God's calendar don't seem to be syncing up. I feel really disappointed because it appears as though He's not coming through. Here's the thing: it's okay to not be okay. It's okay to be disappointed and wonder. There are a lot of people in the Bible who looked at God and said, "I don't have a clue what you're doing. Where are you, God?" And you know what? God had a plan for all of them. And He has one for you and me. Faith is the train ticket that we hold onto while we wait for the train to come.[29]

We need to hold onto it—and wait.

29 Hebrews 11:1

Martha and Mary are very recognizable types. Martha was active and practical, while Mary was introspective and sensitive. Where Mary curled in on herself, Martha got up and did something. Neither was wrong—they were simply different. Martha has been given a bum rap for that one time when she got caught up in her hostess duties and got her priorities mixed up. But she was obviously a solid believer.

When Jesus asked her if she believed He was the resurrection and the life, a pretty heavy question, she didn't hesitate to declare that He was the Messiah, the Son of God. So she knew and believed Him, but she still felt disappointment when He didn't come through for her as she expected. She was about to learn that there's coming through…and then there's really *coming through!*

Maybe neither of those responses resonates with you. Perhaps you identify more with the response of the onlookers. "*But some of them said, 'Could not he who opened the eyes of the blind man have kept this man from dying?'*"[30] This was a response of doubt. These people were not intimates of Jesus, they knew Him only by reputation and hearsay. They had all sorts of different ideas about who and what He was. Perhaps they'd been waiting for the inevitable moment when the celebrity-of-the-moment shows himself to be just another fraud. Does that sound familiar? "Hey, maybe Jesus just isn't who He says He is. I don't know about this whole Messiah thing."

---

30 John 11:37

Maybe, like those in this passage, you've got some questions and you're not really sure. That's okay. God is not afraid of, or offended by, questions. And He's not offended by any of these responses. In fact, such thoughts and feelings are often signposts on the road to the truth.

But don't just notice the response they have towards Jesus, notice the response Jesus has towards them. It's important that you see this side of the Savior. "*Jesus said to her, 'Your brother will rise again.'*"[31] And then when Mary had come to meet him. "*When Jesus saw her weeping and the Jews who had come with her also weeping, he was deeply moved in his spirit and greatly troubled.*"[32] It goes on to say that, "*Jesus wept.*"[33]

What a beautiful Savior!

Here's what Jesus does when we are in pain. He speaks truth and He also sheds tears. He gives hope and He hurts with us. He has conviction and He has compassion. He can meet you right where you are. He knows exactly how to minister to you in your pain, because He has experienced it Himself.

Some people dismiss Christianity. They dismiss God because of the problem of pain. There's so much evil in the world. But they dismiss God because they don't realize that God set aside His deity and became a man, and experienced pain beyond our comprehension. Only Jesus can comfort our pain because only Jesus has entered into our pain and understands it better than we do. No other

31 John 11:23
32 John 11:33
33 John 11:35

belief system, no other religion gives you this. God left His realm and entered fully into ours. He knows our pain. So He can give us hope and hurt with us at the exact same time.

What a loving Savior.

Jesus didn't just join them in their grief, but He turned His attention to the problem because there was still an "elephant in the room." Lazarus was still dead. So Jesus followed the mourners to where they had laid him. "*Then Jesus, deeply moved again, came to the tomb. It was a cave. A stone lay against it. And Jesus said, 'Take away the stone.' Martha, the sister of the dead man, said to him, 'Lord, by this time there will be a bad odor.'*"[34] (In the King James version, it says, "Lord, he stinketh.") Jesus prayed, thanking God for hearing Him, then, "...*he cried out with a loud voice, 'Lazarus, come out.'*" St. Augustine said that had Jesus not used the word "Lazarus," *all* the graves would have opened. Wouldn't that have been a shock for the Pharisees? "*And the man who had died came out. His hands and feet bound with linen strips, his face wrapped with a cloth. And Jesus said to them, 'Unbind him and let him go.'*"[35] Can you imagine the celebration? The excitement? Everybody was happy. They had been weeping and mourning. Now, their brother was alive again.

---

34 John 11:38-39
35 John 11:44

And they celebrated.

That is the story of Lazarus. And you may be thinking, "Okay, that was an entertaining story. But I really don't think that has any relevance at all for my life." If you think that, you could not be more wrong. Jesus not only identified with human *pain*; Jesus solved the human *problem*. Jesus said something, and then He showed something. In order to understand it, you've got to put the little story of Lazarus into the big story of what God is doing in Jesus Christ.

It's all centered around the claim that Jesus made when He was talking with Martha. Did you notice it? Jesus said to her, "*I am the resurrection and the life.*"[36] What a statement! Now you better be able to back that up if you're going to go around making claims like that. What does this even mean? Why is Jesus raising Lazarus from the dead? Is He just showing off? I mean, He just walks in—I've got this really cool trick, I bring dead people back to life. It's an amazing show.

No, he's not showing off at all, though you might think that's what He's doing. You may still be trying to get your mind around the concept that Jesus isn't even showing us here that He's God, (though He is God). He's showing us that He's human. This doesn't have anything to do with His divinity, even though He is fully and eternally divine. Martha said to Jesus, 'Yes, Lord. I believe you are…" the what?

"The Christ."

---

36 John 11:25

Christ, the Son of God who is coming into the world. In other words, she says, "I believe you are the human Messiah. I believe that you are the one promised long ago. I believe that you're the human being anointed of God. You are the Christ." This doesn't have anything to do with His divinity, even though He is fully divine in this moment, as in every moment. This is about His humanity and has huge implications for humanity.

If you are also human, then pay close attention because Jesus was doing something here in the resurrection of Lazarus that has everything to do with your life. Namely, He wasn't talking about you dying.

He was talking about you *living*.

Now you may be thinking, "Here it comes. I knew he'd get here eventually. This is where he inserts the part that asks 'do you have hope when you die?'" Wrong. Jesus said, "Your brother will rise again." And Martha said to Him, "Well, I know he'll rise again in the resurrection on the last day." And Jesus said to her, "*I am the resurrection and the life.*" In other words, here's what Jesus was saying. "Would you stop thinking about the future for a moment? I'm telling you that this is not about the future. This is about right now. This isn't about one day when you die, it's about today as you live. I'm doing something because I *am* the resurrection and the life."

Here's what Jesus is showing us: that in Him, in Jesus, human life is restored. Did you catch that? Human life is restored.

Human beings were created to *live*.

In the first chapters of Genesis, God created humanity, and breathed life into them. He gave them a beautiful setting, amazing food, flowing water, work, abundant blessings, intimate relationship, and in the center of it all, He put the tree of what? *Life.* And He stepped back and looked at it all and He said, "It is very good. This is how it ought to be. This is what I've created humanity to experience."

But humanity turned their backs on God, becoming separated from Him, and that's the condition we all are born into because fallen humanity produces fallen humanity. And the Bible says that we are dead in our trespasses and sins,[37] that the wages of sin is death, that is, separation from God,[38] and that no one seeks after God because all have sinned and fallen short of the glory of God.

I'm not beating you over the head with that. I'm telling you that you were created for more. I'm telling you that's not how it's supposed to be. I'm telling you that you were created to live, really *live*, and to experience fully what it means to be human. That is why Jesus got so upset when He saw that Lazarus had died. He hates the effects of sin on the world, so He raised Lazarus up to show that He can restore your life, for He is the resurrection and the life.

---

37 Ephesians 2:1
38 Romans 6:23

In fact, this is why the Bible so often associates life with Jesus. "I am the way the truth and the..."

Life.[39]

"I am the bread of..."

Life.[40]

"You refuse to come to me that you may have..."

Life.[41]

"I have come that you may have..."

Life.[42]

And life abundantly. Don't you see? Jesus' coming doesn't have anything to do with you dying. It has to do with you living. And that changes everything. It changes the way that you enjoy things in the world. What is it that you enjoy? Sports? Coffee? Here's mine...bread pudding.

It is a gift from God.

The thing is, when I'm not connected to the life source, when I'm not connected with God, when I'm not experiencing all that God has created humanity to be, all I can do is enjoy the thing. But once I have full life in God, I can enjoy not only the *thing*, bread pudding, I can enjoy the *giver* of the thing. It's a deeper pleasure. It's a deeper enjoyment in life that you cannot have apart from Jesus Christ. For whether you eat or drink, do all to the glory of

---

39 John 14:6
40 John 6:35
41 John 5:40
42 John 10:10

God,[43] because you begin to become fully human again, walking through the world in relationship with God, and that changes everything.

It changes how you enjoy the world, it changes how you live in relationships with other people, and it changes the fact that you can have relationship with God. It makes you fully human again. Do you see? The good news of the resurrection is not about dying, it's about *living*.

L'Chaim, to life.

Jesus does this to show us that—in Him—eternal life begins. It is not just human life that is restored, but *eternal* life begins. Jesus' whole point to Martha is to stop thinking about the future. There is going to be a resurrection day, but that is only going to *be* a day because Jesus is there. **Resurrection is wherever Jesus is.** Eternal life is not about a future place. It's about an eternal *person.* It's about Jesus. He is where eternal life begins.

In the Book of Revelation we discover, for instance, that Jesus will return according to His timeline, not ours. When that happens, he's going to wipe away every tear and there will be no more mourning or sorrow. And the Bible says, "Death will be no more."[44]

What did Jesus do in John's Gospel? He returned not according to their timeline, but His. He wiped away their tears and turned their mourning into joy. And death was no more. He let them experience that day what they would one day experience for eternity. Eternal life in Jesus

---

43 I Corinthians 10:31
44 Revelation 21:4

starts today. It's not about one day. It's about today, because it's not about dying, it's about living. And do you understand that this can happen in your life today? If anyone be in Christ they're a new creation.[45]

Paul said that we have been buried in baptism and have been raised to walk in newness of life.[46] Then Peter tells us, "That because of the resurrection of Jesus Christ, we have been born again to a living hope."[47] I can testify to this. That hope, that joy, that peace that is promised to us, we can have right now in our ordinary lives because Jesus is our life.

He has come that you may have life. Jesus not only restores human life, He not only brings in eternal life, but, in Jesus, resurrection life is fulfilled. Lazarus was just the appetizer before the main course. He was the opening band before the headliner music happened.

Lazarus was preparing them for something bigger—something greater. And Jesus knew this. When He raised Lazarus from the dead, He knew exactly what was going to happen. We get a glimpse of it in the text. "So from that day on, they made plans to put him to death."[48] Here's what happened. After Jesus raised Lazarus from the dead, the religious leaders got together and they said, "We can't have this. We're going to have to put a stop to this. We're going to have to kill him."

_____

45 II Corinthians 5:17
46 Roman 6:4
47 I Peter 1:3
48 John 11:53

I wonder if the conversation went like this, "Hey, everybody come here for just a second. I have a great idea. Just hear me out. Why don't we kill the man who keeps giving everybody life?" And yet that's exactly what *religion* does. Religion will strip all of the life out of you. The letter kills but the spirit gives life.[49] Religion takes the life that Jesus gives and crucifies it. But this is not about religion. This is about a real person. His name is Jesus, and you can know Him and you can have a real relationship with Him.

Religion will destroy you. Jesus can resurrect you. But that's not the main point that I want to make. Here's the main point: Jesus knew that to give Lazarus life would mean His death. Jesus knew that to defeat your funeral, He would have to cause His. And He gladly made the trade. Jesus was willing to give His life so that Lazarus could live.

And that's exactly what happened if you follow the narrative of John. On Friday, outside the city they took Jesus out and they nailed Him to a cross. Like Martha and Mary, Jesus felt as though God had abandoned Him. "My God, my God, why have you forsaken me?" But God had a plan. He always has a plan. And they took Jesus' body down off the cross, they laid Him in the tomb for three days, making sure there was no doubt at all that He was dead. And on the third day, the Bible says that as they

---

49 II Corinthians 3:6

came to anoint the dead body, a word was declared to them that would forever change the world. It was declared, "He is not here, for He has risen."

The evidence of the empty tomb, the eyewitness accounts, the actual appearances of Jesus to over 500 people, the unexplainable transformation of the disciples, the impact on human history, and the real experience of millions of Christians throughout the generations give us certainty that Jesus is unquestionably alive and He is most certainly the resurrection and the life.

And what that means for us is that salvation is not about being good or bad, it's about being dead or alive. I know that you might say, "I'm fine because I'm a pretty good person." But, friend, let me be real with you. It's not about being good. It's never been about being good.

One of the most moral people maybe who's ever lived came to Jesus one night. His name was Nicodemus, and he asked Jesus, "How can I enter the kingdom of God? How can I have a relationship with God?" And Jesus didn't say, "Well, try harder." Jesus didn't say, "You need to be a little better." What Jesus said was, "You must be born again," because it's not about being good or bad.

It's about being dead or alive.

Being good didn't get Lazarus out of the grave. Life did. And being good won't get you out of yours, but Jesus can. Jesus gives life. You say, 'Well, how do I get that life?' It's the very question that Jesus asks in this passage. Do you believe? Because whoever believes, lives. Are you alive today? I mean, really alive? Look to Jesus by faith and you will pass from death to life.

Being a Christian, in light of this passage, is not having Jesus as a part of your life. You say, "Really? You don't want Jesus to be a part of my life?" No, I do not want Jesus to be a part of your life because being a Christian is not having Jesus be a part of your life. Being a Christian is having Jesus *as* your life. That's what a Christian is.

Jesus is not an add-on.

He's not a religious blanket to keep you warm in case life gets cold. He is the resurrection and the life, and that means He must be the single defining relationship in your life. You can love other things and love other people. That's good, that's fantastic. Those are gifts from God. But a Christian is someone who has come to the realization that there's nothing better in life than Jesus because He is life. Paul said, "To live is Christ,"[50] and he said, 'Christ who is our life.'[51] Would you look to Him today and trust Him as your very life?

Please know that Jesus is the life you've been looking for. You may have hit dead end after dead end. You might say, "Well, I'm fine. I live for my spouse, I live for my family, I live for my job. I live for fun." But you know that all of those things are temporary. And what will you do when those things are gone? You see, Jesus is the only one who can say, "I will give you everlasting life," and actually deliver. He is the life you're looking for.

Do you remember that famous scene in *Shawshank Redemption* when Andy and Red are out in the courtyard

---

50 Philippians 1:21
51 Colossians 3:4

in the prison, and they're up against the wall? They had a conversation about how life was always going to be that way. They were always going to be in prison. It was never going to change. And eventually, Andy began to get frustrated and he looked at Red, and gave that famous line. "I guess it just comes down to a simple choice. You either get busy living or you get busy dying."

Indeed.

Before you are two options. You can get busy living or you can get busy dying. And I am telling you that Jesus Christ, the resurrection and the life, is the only One who makes the difference.

Abundant life. Eternal life. We choose to live every day with the promise that because Jesus walked out of the grave, we too one day will pass through a grave and we will walk into a kingdom.

And when I get there, I'm going to take my glass, and I'm going to have them fill it all the way up with communion wine. And I'm going to join with the redeemed from every nation in a toast. And I'm going to raise my glass high, and I'm going to look my Savior in the eye, and I'm going to say, "L'Chaim!"

"L'Chaim, to life."

CHAPTER FOUR

Extravagantly Generous

"The apostles gathered around Jesus, and told him all that they had done, and taught. He said to them 'Come away by yourselves to a desolate place, and rest a while,' for many were coming, and going, and they had no leisure even to eat. So they went away in a boat to a desolate place by themselves. But many saw them going, and recognized them, and they ran there on foot from all the towns, and got there ahead of them, and when he went ashore he saw a great crowd, and he had compassion on them because they were like sheep without a shepherd. So he began *to teach them many things. When it grew late his disciples came to him, and said, 'This is a desolate place, and the hour is now late. Send them away to go to the surrounding countryside and villages and buy themselves something to eat.' But he answered to them, 'You give them something to eat.'*

They said to him, 'What... shall we go and buy 200 denari worth of bread, and give it to them to eat?' And, he said to them, 'How many loaves do you have? Go and see.' And, when they had found out they said, 'Five, and two fish.' And then he commanded them to sit down in groups on the green grass. They sat down in groups by hundreds, and by 50s, and taking the five loaves and the two fish he looked up to heaven and said a blessing, and broke the loaves. Then he gave them to the disciples to set before the people, and divided the two fish among them all. And they all ate and were satisfied, and they took up twelve baskets full of broken pieces, and of the fish, and those who ate the loaves were 5,000 men."[52]

You may remember the old fable that was turned into an Oscar-winning film about a small, poor fishing village on

---

52 Mark 6:30-44

the coast of Denmark.[53] In this village lived a very strict religious group. The members wore only black, and their diet consisted of boiled cod and gruel. They avoided any kind of worldly pleasure. They gathered together on their Sabbath, sang hymns, read some passages of Scripture, and thought about heaven. It was very serious, and very strict. The leader of this sect had two daughters. One was named Martine, after Martin Luther, the other was named Philippa, after Philip Melanchthon. They were beautiful women, but very sheltered and never allowed to experience much of life. Neither of them was ever allowed to go to a ball or a party; nor were they allowed to have very many relationships.

Their life was limited to home and to church.

Eventually, Martine fell in love with a military officer, but he soon left to go off to war. Philippa was pursued by a famous opera singer because of her beautiful voice, but she pushed him away. Both women lived very lonely lives. Fifteen years passed. Their sect became smaller, even more strict, and began to split apart. A pair of long-time friends wouldn't speak to each other anymore. A marriage in the group was falling apart. Martine and Philippa were very lonely. They still gathered as a group and sang their songs, but it was dry, empty, and *barren*.

One day there was a knock on the door. A woman stood on the doorstep with a note. Her name was Babette. She had been sent there by the opera singer who loved

---

53 *Babette's Feast*, https://www.imdb.com/title/tt0092603/

Philippa. Babette had lived in Paris, but her husband and son had both died. She had nothing, and she went to the village thinking that maybe they would show her some hospitality. She was an excellent cook, so the daughters agreed to let her live there. She served the family for many years and never asked for anything in return. One day she received a letter informing her that she had won a lottery—10,000 *francs—enough* for her to be able to return home to Paris. But she wasn't sure that was what she wanted. She'd been hearing the daughters talk about a celebration they wanted to have for the hundredth-year anniversary of their group.

She approached the daughters and she asked if she could cook a meal for the celebration. They said, "No, no, no, you don't need to go through all that trouble." She said, "I haven't asked you for anything the entire time I have lived with you. Please, let me do this." They agreed.

Soon, boats started showing up bringing exotic things: champagne, meats, vegetables, truffles. They wondered, "What in the world is Babette up to?" But, they didn't say anything. Finally, the day of the celebration came, and the group walked in to a feast fit for a king. There was expensive wine, duck, roasted pig, cheeses, fruits, and chocolate. They didn't know what to say, and they didn't know what to do. After all, they had been living on boiled cod and gruel.

As they began to eat, they didn't just open their mouths, they opened their lives, and by the time the meal was over, the two friends who hadn't been speaking were reconciled. The couple that had been falling apart was reunited, and faces that hadn't smiled in ages began to laugh. Loneliness was lifted, and they experienced something they had not experienced in a very long time: *satisfaction*.

And they found it in a meal.

That little village was never the same after that day. When the meal was over, the two daughters came up to Babette, and said, "Thank you. By the way, have you decided whether or not you're going to go back home?" She replied, "I'm not going home. I spent everything I had on that meal."

One of the reasons I love that story is because it's such a beautiful example of the kind of real impact extravagant generosity can make, and something about that resonates with us. We've all seen and loved such stories on social media. For instance, Liz Jensen's story. She hardly had enough money to get a wedding dress, and when she showed up one day to take it home, she discovered that a stranger had paid for it. She said, "That kind of stuff happens at a McDonald's drive through, not for a wedding dress." Or, what about James Robertson, an older man from Detroit? He walked 21 miles plus took two bus rides every day just to get to his $10.55 per hour job. It left him with very little time to sleep at night. Somebody found out about it, and they bought him a brand new car.

Beth Hughes was a stay at home mom in Oklahoma. She was about to pay for her Thanksgiving groceries when a customer she didn't even know stepped in front of her and swiped a credit card before she could swipe hers. Or Edgar and Angela Velasquez and family who live in San Raymundo, Guatemala. They have a home today because a church in Minnesota is serious about making a difference in the world. Don't you just love hearing stories about extravagant generosity? The kind of stories where somebody goes the extra mile, does the extra thing, and goes above and beyond to make a difference in somebody else's life? It feels so human. That's because we're created in the image of an extravagantly generous Savior.

That is what we see in the sixth chapter of the gospel of Mark, but in order for us to see the extravagance of our Savior here, we have to see the event in its context. "*When Jesus went ashore he saw a great crowd, and had compassion on them, because they were like sheep without a shepherd.*" Now, my guess is that you have heard this story before of Jesus feeding the multitudes. Perhaps you heard it at Vacation Bible School, or in Sunday school, or maybe in sermons, and the image you have is like this: Jesus at a picnic. You've got all the people sitting around nice and orderly, because that's how crowds behave. There's the little boy so gladly donating his lunch, because that's how children respond when you take food from them. I mean, it's all so pleasant. It's so Sunday school.

And so wrong.

When you envision this story, stop thinking picnic, and start thinking *picketing*. This was not a peaceful gathering for Bible study and banana bread. It was an uprising. This crowd wanted a revolution. How do I know that? First of all, it took place in Galilee, the headquarters of the *Zealot* group, the growing movement that absolutely couldn't stand Roman authority. They despised King Herod, and they wanted to see him overthrown. He had just committed an atrocity and they were fuming mad. Why? If you go back to the verses immediately before our text, you'll see that somebody they loved dearly had just been beheaded. What was his name? John the Baptist. And who gave the order to remove his head? King Herod. So now they were saying, "Enough—this has got to stop."

And who better to overthrow King Herod than King Jesus? "Have you seen His authority? Have you seen His miracles? Do you know what this man can do? Let's go get him, and march Him straight to Herod, and have Him take Herod's head off." Look at what John records about this event, "*Perceiving they were about to come and take him by force to make him king, Jesus withdrew...*"[54] This was a crowd ready for a revolution. There is also a hint in our text in Mark. Jesus sees them "as sheep without a shepherd." That's a direct quote from Moses who says this about Israel desiring a national leader.[55] There's one more clue.

There are 5,000 *men*.

You may have heard that this probably means at least 10,000 people, once you add the women, or even 15,000 or more, if you add the children. That's possible, but not

---

54 John 6:15
55 Numbers 27:17

likely. What is more likely is that this is a description of 5,000 men who are a part of a political revolution. It is not a group of Jewish families out for a Sunday afternoon stroll who just happened to end up hungry. Get that out of your mind. This is a crowd of men who have had enough, and they are ready to use force, they are ready to rise up, they're ready to take over. In fact, they do rise up in revolt not too many years later, and are brutally crushed by Titus. You have to see their anger before you can really see this amazing aspect of our Savior.

But there's another group here to consider besides the multitude of men. Look at the disciples. Remember, they had just returned to Jesus after going about in pairs, preaching and healing the people. Jesus had drawn them away from the crowds and taken them to that desolate place to rest. That, of course, didn't work out and He wound up teaching the crowd for the rest of the day. "*And, when it grew late, his disciples came to him and said, 'This is a remote place and the hour is now late. Send them away to go into the surrounding countryside and villages, and buy themselves something to eat.'*"

I relate with these guys. They'd just come back from doing the ministry Jesus had sent them to do, and they were exhilarated—and exhausted, "I can't wait to tell you what we taught. I can't wait to tell you what we saw. Jesus, you're not going to believe what we experienced. It was incredible, and at the same time, we're so tired. Can we just get away for a little bit?"

The multitude wanted a revolution. The disciples wanted rest, but there was no rest to be had that day.

Have you ever felt that way? Be honest. Has there ever been a conversation, or a situation that you just wanted to avoid because you were tired? If you're a parent, has there ever been a time when you finally got your child to sleep, finally got your baby down... "Oh, finally!" It's been such a long day, and now it is time for you to rest. It's time to lie down, and sleep... and just as soon as you get settled, the baby starts screaming again, and you turn into crazy mom, right? "Enough! I can't handle this right now. He's your kid, not mine!"

Ever felt like that?

Or that co-worker who comes to your cubicle and wants to have that conversation you do not want to have? Have you ever been that way spiritually? "Jesus, I'm just too tired to forgive right now." "I'm too tired to prepare another message." "I'm too tired to serve them in this moment. Can I just have some me time God? Is that too much to ask?"

Listen, the problem is not the desire for rest. The problem is the dependence on self. Jesus is pro rest. He wanted them to rest. That wasn't the problem. The problem was they wanted to rest because they didn't think they could do any more. It was a dependency on self, and guess what? They were right. Jesus was going to push them. Watch what He did. "Jesus answered them, '*You give them something to eat.*'" He pushed them.

"We want rest, send them away, let them feed themselves."

"You feed them."

Which births sarcasm, "Shall we go and buy 200 *denari*—that is eight months' salary-worth of bread for them eat? Come on Jesus. You know we can't do that. Don't you remember how we're provisioned?" They had just returned from their preaching tour for which He'd charged them to take nothing for their journey except a staff. No bread, no bag, and no money in their belts. "Come on. We have no jobs, we have no food. What do you mean we're supposed to feed them?" And then, he pushed them even further. "*And he said to them, 'How many loaves do you have? Go and see.' And when they had found out they said, 'Five, and two fish.'*" Now, you should laugh at that because it is so absurdly inadequate.

What was He doing?

He was teaching them—and us—that we are most useful to Jesus when we admit we're useless *without* Him. He was pushing them. He was forcing them to see that *they couldn't* because He was teaching them that *He can.* What I love here is that Jesus didn't say, "Are you serious? What a joke you guys are. Get out of here." *Poof* - baskets. That's not what He did. What He did was take that laughably insufficient amount of food, thank the Father for it, and then turn it into something so abundant that there were several baskets left over.

Elisabeth Elliot said, 'If the only thing you have to offer God is a broken heart, then offer God a broken heart.' Whatever it is that you have, He can take it, and use it. Jesus wants you to rest, but He will make you restless until you learn you can do nothing apart from Him.

I feel that way a lot of weeks. The sermons my people hear are better than the sermons I prepare, and we *all* have to learn that lesson, not only in the life of a pastor, but in the life of *any* follower of Jesus Christ.

Maturity is not reaching independence, maturity is reaching a greater dependence on Him, and He will push you until you learn that. Having set the disciples up to learn that point, what did He do? "*Taking the five loaves and the two fish, looking up to heaven, he said a blessing and broke the loaves. Then he gave them to his disciples to distribute to the people. He also divided the two fish among them all. They all ate, and were satisfied.*"

The Greek here is imperfect tense, which means that it is continual action. This suggests that Jesus didn't go -*poof* - mounds of bread. It indicates that He broke it, handed it to a disciple who went to set it before the people and came back, and Jesus handed them more, and they went to set it before the people, a continual action. I wonder if they came back thinking, "Well, there can't be any more left. I know what we started with." Yet, every time they came back, they got more, and then more, and still more.

The multiplying took place in the hands of Jesus. It was in His very hands as it was being given that there was more, and more, and more, and more. So, where do you feel inadequate today? What's that thing in your life that has you thinking, "I can't do it. I can't do this." Listen, the good news is—you're right. The better news is—He can. Is it your parenting? Is it forgiving somebody who's hurt you? Is it leadership? Is it something in your finances? Is it being a Christian in this culture? What is it? The truth is that you're never going to get rest until you become restless enough to lay it in His hands.

Not only do we need to learn the lesson that the disciples learned, but we need to see the juxtaposition of two very different attitudes in this scene. The attitude of the multitude was "Let's take over, let's use force, let's conquer." The mindset of the disciples was, "Let's fall back, let's give up, let's quit, we've had enough, let's rest." Then, with those two opposing attitudes clear in your mind, see the beauty of our Savior. Look at how Jesus responded, unlike anybody else in the story.

"When Jesus landed and saw a great crowd, he had compassion on them." Keep in mind that this was right after the death of John the Baptist, Jesus' own cousin. If anything, Jesus had the full emotional right to say, "Not now, paparazzi, get out of here. I'm hurting." But Jesus looked at that crowd, and He had compassion on them. He genuinely cared for them. Not only in feeling, but in action. That is, He felt for them. He gave them spiritual food. The text says He taught them, and then He gave them physical food, that is, fish and bread.

This is what I love about the human side of Jesus. He was not annoyed, He was not irritated, He didn't see them as an interruption on His messianic calendar. He had compassion on them. Do you see that side of your Savior today? Do you know what that means for you? It means that you are not an annoyance to Him. Have you ever felt that way? "I don't really want to pray about this. I don't really want to take this to God, because you know, He's busy, and this is just a First World problem anyway." Then, you begin to rationalize why you're not communing with Christ. Here's what needs to be said: Jesus didn't die on a cross, rise from the dead, ascend to heaven and become your high priest, so that you could justify your lack of prayer by thinking He doesn't care.

He's not looking at you saying, "Her again. I'm so tired of hearing this prayer request. Father, can't we just send her away?" No, no, no. He sees you where you are, even with your false humility, and He has compassion for you. What a Savior! But that has implications. You may say, "I want to experience Jesus every day. My Monday, Tuesday, every day, I want to experience Jesus." You can. You experience Jesus every day when you show compassion to others. When you see it in your Savior, and when you model that by showing compassion to others, you experience Jesus in those moments. You may say, "Well, I'm not Jesus." I'm glad you admit that, but you *are* to be conformed to His image.

Jesus didn't come to conquer politically. He came to inaugurate a kingdom of compassion. By showing compassion to those in your life whom God is bringing to your attention, you'll experience Jesus in the everyday.

But the compassion of Jesus isn't the only thing we are shown in this passage. We also see the *prodigality*, the generosity, of Jesus. *"They all ate, and were satisfied, and the disciples took up twelve baskets full of broken pieces of bread and fish."* Jesus didn't just give, He gave with abundance. He didn't just feed, He fed them until they couldn't eat anymore. How do we know they couldn't eat any more? Because, there were leftovers.

Jesus taught the people of His culture to pray, *"Give us this day our daily bread."* Why? Because they didn't know if they'd have bread tomorrow. In other words, it was a culture where they didn't eat all they could eat, they ate enough to get by, hoping they'd have more tomorrow. So Jesus gave them something many of them had never experienced before—an opportunity to eat until they couldn't eat any more. Then there were leftovers, in a culture that didn't have "doggie bags." What we see here is the *extravagant generosity* of our Savior. Here's what this means for you. Jesus will provide what you need.

It may not be what you want, but it will be what you need. He may let you hunger for a while, but Jesus will feed you, and it *will* satisfy your soul. This also has implications for you. If you want to experience Jesus in the every day, then live generously. Stingy Christians make Jesus look like stale bread. In fact, stingy-Christian is an oxymoron. It doesn't work. How can you close your cupboards when He's filled your stomach? As Christians, we sometimes get hung up on "mine." It's my money, it's my time, and they're my possessions.

Don't ask me to be generous with *mine.*

But if you won't be generous, then you won't be like Jesus. How can we see this side of our Savior and still cling to all that He has given to us? To be generous is to be truly human. You were created in the image of an extravagantly generous Savior. If you want to experience Him in the everyday, then start living generously.

What are you holding onto tightly in your life? Letting go of what Jesus wants you to give will bring such abundance into your life. And if you're giving grudgingly, giving something *extra* will transform your attitude and make a real difference in the lives you touch, including your own.

I've posited that the gospels reveal Jesus in His *humanity*. He set aside His rights and attributes of deity and poured Himself into the *morphe* of humanity. He has been showing us that He's the New Adam, having dominion over the creation, bringing humans back to how we are supposed to live. He cleansed the temple because we were created to worship God. He raised Lazarus because we were created to live, not die. He fed the multitude because, according to Genesis, we were created to live under the provision of a loving God who will feed us with abundance. In other words, He is giving us a glimpse of what it means to experience abundant life under God's provision.

How do we get there? Look at what Jesus did. "*Taking the five loaves and the two fish, looking up to heaven, he said a blessing and broke the loaves.*" Blessing, broke. Does that sound familiar? Have you heard that anywhere else? It sounds exactly like this, *"As they were eating, he took bread and after blessing it, broke it, and gave it to them, and said, 'Take, this is my body.'*[56] Jesus was foreshadowing with the multitude what He was going to do for mankind. He was not only going to break bread, but

---

56 Mark 14:22

He would be broken Himself, and He would die on a cross, and He would rise from the tomb so that you could get back to being human again. So that you could enjoy abundant life in God. So that you would have your soul satisfied forever. That's how you get in, that's how you get back.

You come to Jesus by faith.

I've always loved the story of *Babette's Feast*. To see how one person was willing to give so much just to impact the lives around her. The truth of the matter is, that story is not just a picture of generosity, but it's a picture of the very gospel itself. For the Bible says, "*Though he was rich, for your sake he became poor, so that you through his poverty might become rich.*"[57]

Would you come to a feast today? The one prepared for you in Jesus Christ? Come, eat, believe, and maybe, just maybe, you'll experience something that you haven't experienced in a really long time: satisfaction. Because whoever eats of this bread will never hunger again.

---

57 II Corinthians 8:9

CHAPTER FIVE

Authentically Tempted

"Then Jesus was led by the Spirit into the wilderness to be tempted by the devil. After fasting 40 days and 40 nights, he was hungry. The tempter came to him and said, 'If you are the Son of God, tell these stones to become bread.' But Jesus, answered, 'It is written: Man shall not live on bread alone, but on every word that comes from the mouth of God.' Then the devil took him to the holy city and set him on the pinnacle of the temple. 'If you are the Son of God,' he said, 'throw yourself down. For it is written: 'He will command his angels concerning you, *and they will lift you up in their hands, so that you will not strike your foot against a stone.' Jesus replied, 'It is also written: 'Do not put the Lord your God to the test.' Again the devil took him to a very high mountain and showed him all the kingdoms of the world and their glory. 'All this I will give you,' he said, 'if you will fall down and worship me.' 'Away from me,' Satan, Jesus declared. 'For it is written: worship the Lord your God and serve him only.' Then the devil left him, and angels came and ministered to him."[58]*

Greg Mortenson was an explorer and philanthropist. He loved adventure, nature, and the outdoors. One of his greatest dreams was to climb the world's second tallest mountain—K2. In pursuit of this dream, he traveled to Pakistan and attempted multiple times to get to the top of the great mountain. But even with all of his preparation and dreaming, he failed every time. In his final attempt, he realized he was not going to be able to reach the summit, and he finally admitted defeat, turning back and beginning the trek back down to the base of the mountain.

After wandering without direction, he grew weak from dehydration and exhaustion. Just when he thought he could not go any farther, with no idea of his location, he happened across a remote village. Fortunately, the kind

---

58 Matthew 4:1-11

people of the tiny village took him in and gave him hospitality as well as medical care.

As Greg grew healthier and more aware of his surroundings in the small village, he noticed that there was no school. He was moved with compassion as he realized that with no school, the people of the village had no access to education to provide opportunities necessary to move out of poverty. He decided then and there that he was going to spend the rest of his life building schools to help people who were born into poverty.

He eventually founded the *Central Asia Institute*, a school dedicated to educating young women in remote parts of the world. Women in places such as Pakistan and Afghanistan received education and opportunities that would otherwise have never been available. At one point, Greg was captured by the Taliban and eventually released. He risked sacrificing his own well-being and even his life to make his dream possible.

Greg's inspirational story is written in his autobiographical book, *Three Cups of Tea*, which spent an amazing 220 weeks on the *New York Times* bestseller list. Greg was loved by celebrities, respected by the people in his community, and was even nominated for a *Nobel Peace Prize*. Honor and glory followed him wherever he went. Until, a story broke that changed everything for him.

The truth came out.

While he did do some good over the years, Greg was never captured by the Taliban. Many of the schools that he wrote about establishing never existed. The platform that he had established benefited his wallet more than it helped people. Greg did do some good. But much of the story he told was more idealized fiction than actual fact. When the truth finally came out, and he was finally interviewed about the falsehoods in his book, his reasoning for doing so was striking. When asked why he had fabricated such a story, Greg simply said, "Because of the pressure to be successful in the eyes of others."

Greg did not have an honesty problem, as much as he had an *identity* problem. His failure to be honest and his lack of integrity were outward symptoms of an internal problem. The lack of honesty was the outworking of the identity issue. He felt enormous pressure to be "somebody" in the eyes of other people. His worth was based on what others thought of him. Therefore, he had to present himself in a certain way. His identity shaped his activity.

What we believe about *ourselves* influences the way we live. Behavior is often the outworking of what we perceive our identity to be. In that sense we are all like Greg. This does not mean that we take it to the extreme level that Greg did. We are not all as deceptive or dishonest as he was. But we *are* all searching for identity. We want to be seen in a certain way. The image of ourselves that we project to others, to our children, to our coworkers, to our friends and family is simply the version of self that we want them to see. This is the very thing our enemy uses to lead us into disobedience.

The first way the tempter tempts us is by reshaping our identity. We are all searching for identity. Who am I? Our definition of who we are shapes the way we live our lives. This is important to understand, because when the tempter comes at us, he always goes after who we are. If he can reshape our identity—if he can make us think we are something other than we actually are—then he can very easily lead us astray. That is what the tempter attempted to do to Jesus in Matthew chapter four. Verse three says, *"The tempter came to him and said, 'If you are the Son of God....'"*. Verse six says, *"If you are the Son of God,' he said, 'throw yourself down.'"*

We need to understand what this event in Jesus' life means in the redemptive purposes of God and what Jesus was trying to do in His ministry. The temptation of Jesus was not an accident. It was not random. In fact, Jesus was led by the Spirit into the wilderness to be tempted. This was a divine *appointment*. This event had a purpose in Jesus' life, and it has application for our lives.

So many times when we are walking with Christ we think everything is supposed to go our way. When it doesn't, when trials and temptations hit us out of nowhere, we doubt, worry, rage, and fall. Just as temptation was part of God's will for Jesus, so temptation and trouble are part of us being in the will of God.

Jesus was right where the Father wanted Him to be, in the middle of a wilderness, facing temptation by the tempter himself. The Father allowed Jesus to face this temptation because this was where Jesus started the process of taking humanity back to Eden. He was leading us back to relationship with God. It is important to understand that Jesus, who is the greater Adam, the ultimate human, had to face off against the same serpent that we find way back in the book of Genesis.[59] The serpent came and caused separation between Adam and Eve and God. Humanity fell, and we have been in that fallen state ever since. Jesus came to earth to bring humanity back and it began with Him squaring off with the serpent.

The wilderness account in Matthew's Gospel was a reenactment of the Garden of Eden story in Genesis. The same thing was happening. Jesus was being tempted just as Eve and Adam were tempted. It is important for us to understand the parallels. Adam and Eve were tempted with food. Jesus was tempted with food. Adam and Eve were tempted with power, the ability to be like God. Jesus was tempted with power, the serpent offering Him the kingdoms of the world. Adam and Eve were tempted with false worship. Jesus was tempted with false worship.

It was the same temptation all over again, the timing aligning with the start of Jesus' public ministry. Jesus's ministry was to reconcile God and humanity, so what better place to start than by facing off with the one who caused the separation from the very beginning. This was no coincidence. Rather it was unbelievably significant in the ministry of Jesus.

As this battle happened between the tempter and Jesus, so it often happens in our lives. As mentioned

---

59 See Genesis Chapter Three

earlier, we are tempted to believe a false identity. Satan began with, *"If you are the Son of God...."* Why would the tempter start there? Why would he question Jesus in this way? He did it to cast doubt. Just before this we read, *"When Jesus was baptized, immediately he went up from the water and behold, the heavens were opened to him. He saw the Spirit of God descending like a dove, coming to rest on him. And behold, a voice from heaven said, 'This is my beloved Son, with whom I am well pleased.'"*

In other words, at Jesus' baptism He was declared the Son of God. That is who Jesus is. Then the serpent crept in and began to question that identity. He knows that if he can control the identity, he can control the subsequent activity. And if he can define who we are, or cause us to question who we are, then he can lead us astray. That was exactly what he did with Adam and Eve. They were created in God's image, but the serpent convinced them that they could be even better, that they could like God. What was he doing? He was trying to reshape their identity, telling them that if they ate the fruit that God forbade them to eat, they would be so much more.

As followers of Christ, our identity is in Him. The demonic powers of this world do not care if we think highly of ourselves or lowly of ourselves as long as we do not see ourselves for who we actually are in Christ. The serpent wants to reshape our identity as beloved sons and daughters of Christ. He wants us to question our identity in Christ. He wants us to doubt our identity in Christ. He wants us to forget that our identity is found in Christ. If he succeeds, he can easily lead us astray. He succeeds by convincing us that our lives are special. That we deserve more. That we have somehow earned and are owed special recognition. Or he will go in the other direction and convince us that we are worthless and our situation is hopeless. That we are victims and are weak, that we cannot say no.

One of the lies of the serpent is that we cannot help being a certain way. "It's just who I am," we say. All of these are ways that the serpent tries to get us to believe in a false identity. This is why we need to always remember the gospel. We need to have a *gospel identity*. The gospel identity will not let us say, "I deserve this." If we have a gospel identity, we know that because of our sin we deserve hell. The gospel identity will not let us say, "I'm worthless." According to the gospel we are radically loved children of God. The gospel allows us to maintain a proper perspective of identity in Christ so that we can walk in obedience.

There is an old movie called, *The Elephant Man*. In this movie a man is disfigured because of a disease, and because of his disfigured appearance, his parents gave him away. They wanted nothing to do with him. It is heartbreaking. In one particular scene this man is sitting at a table with some friends drinking tea. As he looks around the table at his friends he says, "If only my mother could see me with friends. Maybe then she would love me. I was such a disappointment to her."

Who do we let define us? Is it the voice from heaven? Or is it the voice in the wilderness? Who do we let define our identity? We have an enemy that hates us so much that he will do anything in his power, using any method available, to reshape the way we think about ourselves and our lives. His aim is to take our eyes off of the truth of God and lead us astray. He tried to tempt Jesus to believe a false identity.

But he went even further.

He also wanted Jesus to act on counterfeit desires in three different ways:

> "After fasting 40 days and 40 nights, he was hungry. The tempter came to him and said, 'If you are the Son of God, tell these stones to become bread.'"

> "Then the devil took him to the holy city, and set him on the pinnacle of the temple. 'If you are the Son of God,' he said, 'throw yourself down. For it is written: 'He will command his angels concerning you, and they will lift you up in their hands, so that you will not strike your foot against a stone.'"

> "Again the devil took him to a very high mountain and showed Him all the kingdoms of the world and their glory. 'All this I will give you' he said, 'if you will fall down and worship me.'"

Why did the devil tempt Jesus with those specific things? First, humanity was created to eat. This was true in Genesis when God told Adam and Eve that they could eat of any tree in the garden except for one. Second, humanity was created for dominion. God gave humans dominion over the air and the fish of the sea. And third, humanity was created to worship God, as we were created in His image.

Here is the point. All of these desires, the desire for food, the desire for dominion, and the desire to worship, were good. It is a good thing to eat. It is a good thing to have dominion over the creatures of the world. It is a good thing to worship God. The desire for these things was given to humanity by God, and the fulfillment of these desires comes from God. But the enemy takes those God-given desires and he twists them so that we desire these things, not from God, but from ourselves or others. We get what God has promised us in a way that God has not promised. For example, the tempter will use the desire for sex, a God-created and God-given desire, and he will twist it so that we desire it out of God's holy and perfect parameters. He will take our desire for success, and twist it so that we are defined by how far we go and how much we do.

From the beginning the serpent has said, "Eat. You were created to eat. You deserve food. But not for the glory of God. Eat to satisfy the appetite; to fill the stomach." The tempter knows where to strike first. He knows our weakness. When he tempted Jesus he chose food first because he knew that Jesus had not eaten in 40 days and was hungry. The tempter found Jesus' natural and physical weakness and used it to tempt Him. James said, *"But each person is tempted when he is lured and enticed by his own desire. And then desire, when it is conceived, gives birth to sin. And sin, when it is fully grown, brings forth death."*[60]

A great illustration for this is fishing. I love fishing. Good fishermen know what fish like to eat. They know how to take something that is artificial and make it look very real. They also know how to hide the hook where the fish cannot see it. Eventually the fish becomes lured away by the very natural desire of hunger, and when it bites, it finds itself hooked and is led away to death. That is exactly what the tempter did to Adam and Eve. It is what he tried to do to Jesus. It is what he does with us. He takes natural desires in us and he twists the desire in a way that is not of God. It looks like the real thing, but underneath is pain and destruction. When we bite, we find ourselves hooked and are led away. This is the way of the tempter. Since the garden he has been tempting humanity in this way. He wants us to believe a false identity so that he can control our activity.

He wants us to act on counterfeit desires.

Notice that the tempter tried to get Jesus to focus on the now, and not the later. Jesus was hungry, NOW. Jesus could prove He was God, NOW. Jesus could have all the kingdoms of the world, NOW. But everything that the tempter used to tempt Jesus was a promise of God that Jesus would eventually have. Jesus knew He would eat again. Jesus knew that He would have a name that is above every name. Jesus knew that at the name of Jesus

---

60 James 1:14

every knee will bow and tongue will confess. In other words, He was going to get all the glory that the devil offered to Him, in God's timing, according to His will.

The tempter tried to distract Jesus from the future promises of His Father. He tried to convince Him that He didn't need to go through the pain and suffering of death on a cross when He could have all the food, kingdoms, and glory now. He did the same in the garden and he does the same to us now. He offers immediate gratification and immediate rewards. He offers a temptation of pleasures now, even though we have the promise of God for eternity. Jesus offers us the example of how to respond to these false promises. Jesus refused to bow.

Matthew recorded Jesus' responses:

> *"But Jesus answered, 'It is written: Man shall not live on bread alone, but on every word that comes from the mouth of God.'"*

> *"Jesus replied, 'It is also written: Do not put the Lord your God to the test.'"*

> *"'Away from me, Satan,' Jesus declared. 'For it is written: Worship the Lord your God and serve him only.'"*

Every time the tempter came at Jesus, Jesus refused to give in. This is really important because it relates to the message of the gospel, which is not just that Jesus came, died, and rose again. The gospel also tells us that He lived a perfect, sinless life, so that He would be our perfect, spotless sacrifice. When faced with temptation, Jesus did not bow. He did not give in.

Jesus was authentically tempted. He was tempted in the same manner that Adam and Eve were tempted. He was tempted in the same way that the tempter tempts us today. Sometimes we like to believe that Jesus was a type of superman while He lived on the earth, as if He could not feel hunger, pain, or desire, and was immune to temptation. But that is not how the author of Hebrews portrays Him. Hebrews 4:15 says, *"We do not have a high priest who is unable to sympathize with our weaknesses, but one who in every respect has been tempted as we are, and yet without sin."*

Jesus was truly tempted, just as we are today. His temptation was authentic. Jesus felt real pressure. He perceived real crisis. His physical hunger and weakness was real. This often makes me ponder whether or not Jesus, in these moments, could have sinned. Could He have given in to the temptation of the devil? Could He have turned the stones into bread? Many people believe that He could have sinned, but He did not. This, they say, is how they know it was an authentic temptation. He chose to obey His father over any temptation He faced. I believe that Jesus could not have sinned, because although He was fully human, He was also fully God. Does this make the temptation less authentic and Jesus reaction to temptation any less applicable to our lives? When we focus on whether or not Jesus could have sinned, we are taking our focus off of the humanity of

Jesus, and how we need to think about our Savior as He was being tempted.

As an illustration, imagine a swimmer whose goal is to break the world record for the longest swim. As the swimmer trains, he swims short distances on some days, and longer distances on other days. He notices that during the longer swims he experiences debilitating muscle cramps, his body is fatigued, and he begins to fear that he may drown during the race. He consults with his friends and they decide that when he swims long distances they will follow about thirty feet behind him, ensuring that he will not drown.

On the day of the swim, the swimmer dives into the water and begins to swim. He becomes fatigued. He is exhausted. There is pressure. He really feels all of these things, but he still goes on to break the world record. Could the swimmer have drowned? The answer is no, because the boat was always there to rescue him. But the boat did not keep him from drowning. The swimmer staying vigilant even in the midst of physical suffering is what ensured his success. He knew the boat was there, so he was able to swim all the way to the end, regardless of how he felt, with no fear of drowning.

Jesus could not have sinned. There was no chance of Jesus failing during temptation because of His divinity. But that is not why He did not sin. He did not sin because, in His humanity, He used all the resources given to Him. This is great news for human beings today! As followers of Christ we have access to the same resources that Jesus had. We have the word of God, the Holy Spirit, and the certainty of the promises of God that we will not be tempted beyond what we can bear.[61] God is our friend in the boat.

Jesus could not have sinned because of His divinity, but this is a completely separate issue from the reason He did not sin. He did not sin because, as the greater Adam, as the ultimate human, He did what Adam did not do. He walked in complete faithfulness to God. Without this truth, He could not restore humanity back to God. He was fully human, fully man, who meditated on God's word. Every time He was tempted He responded, "It is written...." He didn't respond by revealing His divinity. Rather, He responded in humanity, by knowing and using the Word of God in the midst of temptation to walk in faithfulness to His Father. He depended on the Holy Spirit.

Jesus was authentically tempted for us. He faced pressure. He faced hardship. He faced exhaustion. He faced physical hunger. We need to understand that the temptation Jesus experienced in the wilderness was real, and, for us, He swam all the way to the end so that we could be restored in relationship with God.

What does this mean for us?

First, the Apostle Peter wrote, *"Beloved, don't be surprised at the fiery trial when it comes upon you to test you as though something strange were happening to you. Rejoice in so far as you share Christ's sufferings that you may also rejoice and be glad when His glory is revealed."*[62]

---

61 I Corinthians 10:13
62 I Peter 4:12

Second, we should never minimize or fail to use the resources we have in Christ. The swimmer used the resources available to him and was successful. Jesus was successful in His human temptation because He used His God-given resources. Why? So that it would encourage us that we can also walk in obedience. We have scripture to guide us. We have Jesus, our high priest, to give us strength. We have the Holy Spirit living inside us, guiding and directing us. We have a loving Father who provides for us. We have the body of Christ, the church, to offer help, community and support. We have prayer, a direct connection to God, to sustain us. We may face temptation in the wilderness, but we are never alone. We have the power of the Almighty God on our side. We have the resources to fight in the war against the devil that we face every day.

Third, in our humanity on this earth, we know that we have all sinned. So many of us use the excuse, "I'm only human" to justify failing to obey God. But Jesus' temptation gives us confidence that when we follow His example, and apply these truths to our lives, we, like Jesus, can walk in obedience with our Father. Jesus, the true human, did not sin. Adam, the human created in the beginning, was created to walk in obedience to God.

We need to remember that in God's eternal kingdom, and in the final day, we will experience resurrection and restoration of our sinful and broken bodies and lives. We will be restored to the humanity that God intended. We will be human forever, and we will not be able to sin. To be human is to walk in obedience to God. Sin is subhuman.

Humanity was created by God, for God, to walk with God in righteousness, just as Jesus did in the wilderness.

Finally, when we look at this side of our Savior, we can experience Jesus in our everyday lives. When we walk in obedience, we are becoming more like Jesus, the perfect, sinless human. When we are on the computer, when we are driving on the interstate, when we are doing dishes or cleaning the house, in whatever situation we are in, there is a war raging: the war between our sinful desires to which the tempter wants us to succumb, and the perfect path of obedience to our Father. Jesus experienced this temptation in His life and He chose to walk in obedience. We can experience Jesus in our lives when we choose His ways instead of our own.

Greg Mortenson was not the first person to have a kingdom crumble because of a false identity. And he won't be the last. That reality began in the garden, when a smooth talking serpent seductively convinced humanity to look outside of God for identity. As a result, humanity was driven out of the garden and separated from God. We have been searching for identity ever since. But there is good news. The good news is that God so loved the world He sent His only Son, not just into the world, but into a wilderness to be authentically tempted in our place. And there, He defeated the one who defeated us and He is bringing us back to God.

CHAPTER SIX

Totally Surrendered

"Then Jesus went with his disciples to a place called Gethsemane, and he said to them, 'Sit here while I go over there and pray.' He took Peter and the two sons of Zebedee along with him, and he began to be sorrowful and troubled. Then he said to them, 'My soul is overwhelmed with sorrow to the point of death. Stay here and keep watch with me.'

"Going a little farther, he fell with his face to the ground and prayed, 'My Father, if it is possible, may this cup be taken from me. Yet, not as I will, *but as you will.' Then he returned to his disciples and found them sleeping. 'Couldn't you men keep watch with me for one hour?' he asked Peter. 'Watch and pray so that you will not fall into temptation. The spirit is willing, but the flesh is weak.'*

"He went away a second time and prayed, 'My Father, if it is not possible for this cup to be taken away unless I drink it, may your will be done.' When he came back, he again found them sleeping, because their eyes were heavy. So he left them and went away once more and prayed the third time saying the same thing. Then he returned to the disciples and said to them, 'Are you still sleeping and resting? Look, the hour has come, and the Son of Man is delivered into the hands of sinners. Rise! Let us go! Here comes my betrayer!'"[63]

A moment that the world of golf will always remember took place at the historic Carnoustie Golf Club in Scotland in 1999. Carnoustie was the home of the British Open that year, and what made it so memorable, so historic was a Frenchman by the name of Jean van de Velde. When he came to the 18th hole on the final day of the tournament, he was well in the lead, literally 480 yards away from his

---

63 Matthew 26:36-46

first major championship, a huge purse, a trophy with his name on it, and his name etched into the annals of golf. When he walked up to the 18th tee on that last day, his lead was so big that he could make a double bogey and still win the tournament. That's two strokes over par if you don't follow golf. Anyone can double bogey. I mean, *I* can double bogey. I've double bogeyed a lot of times in my golf career. It is not difficult. All he had to do was take his six, smile for the cameras, get his trophy and his money, and walk off into the sunset.

He stepped up to the 18th tee and he grabbed his driver. Even the announcer was saying, "That's not the right club." There was no reason for him to use a driver on that hole, but he did, and the obvious happened.

"Uh-oh. Oh, Oh, you lucky little rascal. That bounced and seemed to go away to the right."

So he pushed his drive, but he got away with it. No reason to panic. He had 240 yards left and plenty of strokes to spare. All he had to do was to hit a nice simple shot onto the fairway. But whatever else, not go for the green.

He pulled out his two iron and went for the green.

"Did he hit the bunkers? First tee. I don't believe this. What is going on here?"

Jean had gotten into grass so tall it could cover the refrigerator in a redneck's front yard. I mean, he was in big time trouble, but he still had plenty of strokes. Still no need to panic—just take a deep breath. All he had to do was lay up. Just hit a nice easy shot back into the fairway but, for goodness sake, do *not* go for the green.

He went for the green.

"It's under the green? Yeah, it must be. I don't believe it. This is..."

Now he was in the water. But even so, he had a big enough lead that he still had the strokes to spare. All he had to do was to take his drop, lose a stroke, get up and down, and he'd still be the British Open Champion. Whatever else he chose to do, he couldn't try to play it from the water.

"We've all seen a few miscues and mishaps in our golfing careers, but oh, Jean, Jean, Jean. What are you doing? What on Earth are you doing? No, Jean, please. Would somebody kindly go and stop him? Give him a large brandy and knock him down."

I think we can agree that when the announcer is ordering you an alcoholic beverage, you are in bad shape. "Would somebody just go stop him?" Well, he did come to his senses and take the drop, but his next shot ended up in the sand. Long story short, van de Velde ended up with a triple bogey, forced a playoff, and lost the championship.

They say golf is a lot like spandex shorts: it tends to reveal things about you most people don't want to see. But the truth of the matter is that most of us can relate to him. I don't mean that you've lost a major championship on the final hole. I mean that you can relate to being in a situation where you refused to surrender your pride. You refused to do it any other way but your way. You relied way too much on your own strength (or knowledge or experience) and you ended up making a mess. Can you relate to that?

It goes like this. All you had to do was to say, "I'm sorry," but no, no, no, no, no. You had to pull the driver out of your bag and cause an argument. All you had to do was to keep your big mouth shut, but no, you had to pull out the two iron and get the last word. All you needed was just a little bit of patience, a little bit of restraint, but no, no, no. You had to go for the green and take control. All you had to do was just let it be, but you had to send that email anyway. All you had to do was surrender to God, but not you. You had to do it your way.

Why is it so hard to leave the driver in the bag? Answer: pride, pride, pride. One author said it this way, "Most Americans believe a few simple propositions: Choice is a good thing and the more you have it, the better you are. Authority is inherently suspect, and no one should have the right to tell others how to think or behave." In other words, we Americans love our independence, and we think the more independence we have, the happier we will be.

But this is what we have to wrap our mind around. Self-reliance may be American, but it is not human. It may be what we value, it may be good socially, but it isn't human.

Humanity was not created to rely on self. Humanity was created to rely on God. Human beings, all of us, were not created to rely on self, not meant to depend upon our own strength. We were created from the very beginning to live surrendered, to willingly live in submission to a good and faithful and loving God.

That is *exactly* what we see in our Savior here in Matthew's account. Look at it. It is beautiful. Jesus went with His disciples to a place called Gethsemane. He told them to sit there while He went over there to pray. He took His three closest with him, Peter, James, and John, and He shared the turmoil He was going through. He told them, "My soul is overwhelmed with sorrow, even to the point of death. Remain here and watch with me.'"

You know the context, this happened immediately after the institution of the Lord's Supper in the upper room. It was right before Jesus was betrayed and arrested, He knew it was coming and He was there in the Garden of Gethsemane with His closest followers, the ones that He, Himself, chose. He left most of them in one place and walked a little apart with His three dearest and as He walked away, the text says, something really hit Him.

Has something ever hit you? You were just going along and all of a sudden you felt weak? All of a sudden you got dizzy or a sick feeling? Like somebody just flipped a switch and something overwhelmed you? At that moment, something overwhelmed Jesus so that He was distressed to the point of death. A shock of terror shot through Him. He was sorrowful, afflicted beyond measure. He was troubled. An internal conflict raged in Him.

In Luke's account, we discover that it was so bad that, "...*an angel from heaven appeared to him and strengthened him. And being in anguish, he prayed more earnestly, and his sweat was like drops of blood falling down to the ground.*"[64]

Most of us know this story, but this isn't how we tend to think about Jesus. We don't want to think of Jesus as weak. We prefer to think of His strength. We think of Jesus making the lame walk, not being unable to walk Himself. We like to think of Jesus celebrating the Passover, not agonizing and in intense sorrow.

What caused Jesus to experience this turmoil in Matthew's gospel? Some have suggested that the reality of the cross was starting to set in, that He was beginning to realize His imminent death. But I don't think that's the case at all. Jesus had already talked about His death very openly, even in the first verse of this chapter. "*When Jesus had finished saying all these things, he said to his disciples, 'As you know, the Passover is two days away— and the Son of Man will be handed over to be crucified.*'" And later, during the Lord's Supper, "*This is my blood of the covenant, which is poured out for many for the forgiveness of sins.*" I don't think Jesus was upset about the crucifixion. He was very well aware of that. He'd been talking openly about it. That wasn't what hit Him.

Others say it was the realization that He was about to be betrayed by His closest friends. The people that He'd entrusted himself to, that he'd done ministry with, were about to stab Him in the back. But Jesus was open about that as well. When Peter told Him, "*Though they all fall away because of you, I will never fall away,*" Jesus said to

64 Luke 2:43

him, "*Truly, I tell you this very night before the rooster crows, you will deny me three times.*" Jesus was very open about it, so what was causing His anguish? Why so much sorrow?

Jesus, Himself, tells us what is troubling Him. "*Going a little farther, he fell with his face to the ground and prayed, 'My Father, if it is possible, may this cup be taken from me.*" Let this cup pass from me. In other words, Jesus was not feeling anguish because of a cross. He wasn't feeling anguished because of the betrayal of close friends. It was something about this "cup." In fact, Jesus was asking the Father, "Is there a way to accomplish the cross without drinking the cup? Can we have a cross without the cup?"

What was the cup? Isaiah tells us, "*Awake, awake! Rise up, Jerusalem, you who have drunk from the hand of the Lord the cup of his wrath....*"[65] And Jeremiah tells us, "*This is what the Lord, the God of Israel, said to me, 'Take from my hand this cup filled with the wine of my wrath, and make all the nations to whom I send you drink it.*"[66] And John wrote in Revelation, "*...they, too, will drink the wine of God's fury, which has been poured full strength into the cup of his wrath.*"[67]

The "cup" was the wrath of God, the wrath of His Father. As Jesus was walking away from the disciples, what came upon Him was not, "Oh, I'm about to be betrayed." Oh, no, no, no. It was not, "Oh, I'm about to go

---

65 Isaiah 51:17
66 Jeremiah 25:15
67 Revelation 14:10

through the agony of crucifixion." No. Those things were not what ultimately dismayed Jesus. It was not just the fact that He was about to face death, or that He was about to be physically beaten, or that He would be betrayed by His close friend. It was that He would drink the cup of the all-consuming wrath of His Father; that the One who knew no sin would be made to *be* sin, making Him the target of His Father's condemnation.

Paul said, "*For God put Christ forth as a sacrifice for our sins to prove that he is just, and the justifier of the one who has faith in him*." The very thought of even drinking a drop of that cup almost killed Jesus in the garden. He pleaded, "Father, can we have a cross without a cup? Is there another way? Can the cup pass?"

I wonder what that dialogue must have been like. Oh, what wouldn't I give to have heard that conversation between the Son and the Father. What did the Father say to the Son in this moment? The text doesn't say. Anything that we might come up with would be speculation except that we know this much: that God so loved *you* that He said, "No, it cannot pass. You must drink every drop."

Was Jesus' response, "But I've got rights. No way. I'll do it my way. I'll do my own thing. I'll do my own will. I will rely on myself."? No. Had Jesus said that, you'd be destined for Hell right now. Instead Jesus said, "My Father, if it is possible, let this cup pass from me. Nevertheless, not as I will, but as you will." He said it's not about me. It's not about what I want. It's what You will. Later He said, "*My Father, if it is not possible for this cup to be taken away unless I drink it, may your will be done*."

This is not some kind of empty rhetoric, not a nice cliché to add on to the end of a prayer to make it sound spiritual. Jesus was really struggling. He was really, dreadfully afraid. The One who had been in eternal communion with the Father was about to face the Father's wrath. He was weak, He was in agony, and yet, in it all, He surrendered. He offered total surrender to the Father.

You are intended to see in the text the contrast of that with the disciples. Look back, for instance, to Peter's response to Jesus[68]... By the way, talk about always taking the driver out of the bag. That's Peter. "I know I'm on the green, but I think driver would be perfect because I can do this. It's all about my strength." Listen. What does he say? "*If they all fall away, I never will*," because I'm American. I can rely on me. I can do it in my strength. I've got this.

Then look at what happens in the garden: *"He came to the disciples and found them sleeping, and he said to Peter, 'So you could not watch with me one hour?'"* What happened to all of that "do it yourself?" What happened to all that strength you had? You said you could do this, and you couldn't even make it an hour.

You've got to see the contrast. The disciples think they're strong, so they depend on their strength, only to prove how weak they really are. Jesus is truly weak, and He surrenders to the Father and finds strength. You've got to see that contrast. The ones that think they're strong get

---

68 Matthew 28:33-34

proven to be weak, and the one who's weak yet surrenders to the Father finds strength.

In the hour of His greatest crisis, deepest sorrow, the moment of His most intense agony, Jesus knew that the position of strength is the one of surrender.

How could Jesus do this? How could He be so totally surrendered to the Father in this moment? Well, I would argue this, that Jesus was surrendered at the end because He was totally surrendered all along. Listen to how Jesus describes His life. I wonder if you would describe your life in a similar way.

> *"Jesus said to them, 'My food is to do the will of him who sent me and to accomplish his work. My life is not about me. It's about the Father and what the Father has given me to do."[69]*

> *"For I have come down from heaven not to do my will, but the will of him who sent me."[70]*

> *"But I do as the Father has commanded me, so that the world may know that I love the Father."[71]*

I want the world to know I love the Father. I want to speak on behalf of the Father. I want to do what the Father

---

69 John 4:43
70 John 6:38
71 John 14:31

wants me to do. I want to fulfill all that the Father has commanded. I want the world to know I live surrendered.

Peter will say it this way about Jesus, "*When he was reviled, he didn't revile in return. When he suffered, he didn't threaten, but he continued entrusting himself to him who judges justly.*"[72]

You may be saying, "Well, yeah, but Jesus is God. Of course He surrenders." Yeah, but this isn't about His divinity. He is God. He's fully God, eternally God, but this isn't about His divinity. This is about His humanity.

But, what does surrender have to do with humanity? Why have I been saying stuff like self-reliance may be American, but it's not human? Here's why. Because in the very beginning, in the book of Genesis, humanity was not created to live according to their own way. They were created to live God's way. In fact, it was their lack of submission, it was their self-reliance, it was their unwillingness to surrender that brought sin in. The thing that made a mess of everything was them saying, "We're going to do it our way. We're going to rely on our own wisdom... We want independence." But we weren't created to live that way. We weren't created to find joy there. We weren't created to find peace there, because what it means to be human since the very beginning of humanity is living surrendered to God.

Think about the parallels here between the first Adam in Genesis and the ultimate Adam, the ultimate human, Jesus. Adam was put in a garden. He's told to obey

---

72 I Peter 2:23

about a tree, that is: don't eat. If he obeys, he lives; but he refuses to surrender. Jesus was put in a garden. He's told to obey about a tree, the cross. If He obeys, He will die but you will live—and He surrenders. "Not my will, but Yours."

Here's the contrast. Adam lived *my* will be done. Jesus lived *Your* will be done, because that's what it means to be truly human. It is why Jesus says this. "*If anyone would come after me, let him deny himself, surrender all, and take up his cross and follow me. For whoever would save his life is going to lose it, but whoever loses his life for my sake is going to find it.*"[73] In other words, Jesus is saying, "Do you really want life? Do you want real life? It comes through surrender."

Self-reliance leads to death. Surrendering to Jesus brings life. It's why He taught us to pray this way: "*'Our Father in heaven, hallowed be your name, your kingdom come,* **your will be done**.'"[74] Say that out loud. Did you feel human in that moment? You should, because that's how you were created to live. Not my will but "*Your will be done on Earth as it is in heaven.*"

Prayer is not only an act of worship, it is an act of surrender to God. It is a recognition, a good, joyful, peaceful, human recognition that says, "I can't rule my money. I can't rule my marriage. I can't make decisions. I can't lead a church. I can't run a business. I can't love my kids. I can't do any of that in my own strength. I need You.

---

73 Matthew 16:24-25
74 Matthew 6:9

I surrender. While I remain active in those things, I'm trusting You. I want to do this for You. I want to do this with the strength that You provide me. I want Your will to be done in my life."

That's human. That is what we see in our Savior. Gary Thomas said, "Christian health is not defined by how happy you are, or how prosperous you are, or how many people you've led to the Lord this past year. Christian health is ultimately defined by how sincerely we wave the flag of surrender."[75] Christian health. Do you want to know if you're healthy spiritually? It's defined by how sincerely we wave the flag of surrender.

Charles Stanley put it this way. "Surrender for a general means defeat, but surrender for the Christian is victory."[76] Amen. Surrender for the Christian is victory.

What is it today that you need to surrender? Perhaps you've never surrendered your life to God. You've never stepped down off the throne of your life to say, "I can't do this. I don't want to do this anymore. I turn from my sin and I say, 'Jesus, would You be King? Would you be Lord of my life?' I surrender to You today."

Or perhaps you are a Christian but there are areas in your life that you're trying to do entirely on your own strength. You are pulling the driver out of the bag every time. "I got this. I'll do this," and you wonder why things are such a mess. Maybe you're still trying to earn God's love, and you think that what you do defines how much

---

75 Gary Thomas, Seeking the Face of God
76 Sermon Unconditional Surrender part 1

He loves you. You just need to realize that He drank the cup so that you could enjoy God's love and know that it is finished. You don't have to earn His love. You can surrender and receive it. What is it today in your life or about your life that you need to say, "Not my will but Yours be done"?

I am never going to be able to relate to what it's like for Peyton Manning to throw a football. I'm never going to be able to understand or relate to what it's like for LeBron James to shoot a basketball. But there's one person I can relate to: van de Velde. I totally can relate to him, because I know what it's like to be on the fairway of life doing things my own way. I know what it's like, and I bet you do too, to rely way too much on my own strength, only to make a mess of things.

Here's my challenge. Let's be a little less American and a little more human, a little less self-reliant and a little more totally-surrendered. Let's be like our Savior, a man who lived the human life from beginning to end, not with the mindset of my will be done, but with a mindset of God's will be done.

CHAPTER SEVEN

Intimately Present

> *"Rising very early in the morning while it was still dark, Jesus departed and went out to a desolate place, and there he prayed."*[77]

A 63-year-old woman sat in a chair in the middle of a large room. In front of her was a very plain desk with nothing on it. On the other side of the desk was an empty chair. She sat there, head down, eyes closed. A young man walked into the room and sat down in the empty chair. He was

---

77 Mark 1:35

visibly nervous. His hands were shaking. He was bouncing his legs. He looked down at the floor, back up at the ceiling, around the room. He was obviously nervous.

After a few moments, she raised her head, opened her eyes, and for the next four minutes, though it felt like forever, stared into his eyes. No words were spoken. They just looked at each other. His body froze. All that nervous energy was gone. Tears began to stream down his face, and hers as well. After a time, he smiled as if to say thank you and he walked out of the room.

That exchange, or at least an exchange very similar to that, took place with that same woman and more than 1,500 people, over a total of 700 hours, during a period from the middle of March to the end of May, all in the Museum of Modern Art in New York City. It was an event entitled *The Artist is Present*, and the whole idea behind the event was to stage a live protest against the lack of human connection that takes place in our society. It was to create a place where, no matter who you were or what your background, you could come to a place and make actual human contact.

The response to this event was overwhelming. Word of it spread throughout New York City, a city known for its crowded loneliness. It moved people to tears. Some people even got tattoos to memorialize the moment. Some said they had epiphanies. Some said they regained hope. Some said it was the first time I felt human.

You see, that experiment actually revealed something about human beings: We were created for presence. We were created to be present. You and I know that in our culture, in our lives, we are constantly pulled away from being present. Technology, for all of its many benefits, has created an illusion of presence when most of the time we're anything but. There's always a screen to click, updates to check, tweets to send, schedules to keep, and images to maintain. Our lives, if we would stop and take inventory, are filled with siren calls luring our attention and distracting our focus.

The result of it is that we lose a sense of real presence. We take pictures of sunsets that we don't stop to enjoy. We have lots of friends whom we don't actually know. We're at home thinking about work, and we're at work thinking about home. We're texting when we ought to be driving. We replace real spouses with pornographic images. We are obsessed with the green grass of the future to the neglect of the ripe fields of the present.

Sadly, it usually takes a crisis in life to wake us up. The loss of a loved one, the end of a relationship, a health crisis to wake us up to the reality that, most of the time, we're living on autopilot. We've lost the sense of real presence in life.

There are many applications to this. We could talk about being present with family, being present at work, being present at church, being present in relationships, but I want to talk about the most important one of all. How often in the fast flowing current of your life are you just present with God? I don't mean that you sit at the table and gaze into the face of another human being. Oh, that's important. That's significant. What I'm asking is, are there times in your life where you stop and gaze on the beauty of God, where you stop and think about the glory of God, where you stop and meditate on the truth of God, where you are actually present with God?

One author pointed out, "In the digital age, it may be the case that the classical debates about the presence of Jesus and the sacraments have been inverted. That is, the question is no longer in what way is the Lord present at the supper? The real question is, in what ways are we?"

This intentional presence, this consistent pursuit of communion with God is a side of the Savior we see throughout the gospels. Look at that verse in Mark again. "*Rising very early in the morning while it was still dark, Jesus departed and went outside to a desolate place, and there he prayed.*" What's the context of this occasion? Go back a few verses. "*That evening at sundown, they brought to Jesus all who were sick and oppressed by demons, and the whole city was gathered together at the door. And He healed many who were sick with various diseases and cast out many demons, and he would not permit the demons to speak because they knew him.*"[78] That's what Jesus was doing the night before He rose early in the morning to be alone with God.

Has work ever taken you into the night? Not only that, the text says that everybody in the town was at His doorstep. That was a lot of need. There were a lot of issues. Add to that the fact that Jesus was engaging in spiritual warfare. He was casting out demons. Now, we tend to think that Jesus did this effortlessly. You know, He was

---

78 Mark 1:32

just like, "Demon, out. Demon, out. Somebody go get me a latte at Starbucks. Demon, out. Demon, out." As though He casually - ho-hum - flicked them off like bugs....

Might I remind you that spiritual warfare is exhausting. You remember how Jesus was in the wilderness when He was tempted. I assure you, fighting demons is more exhausting than mowing grass, than chasing children all day, than running marathons.

Remember, also, that Jesus had set aside the attributes of His divinity and was doing this in His humanity. He was fully God, eternally God, but Paul told us in his letter to the Philippians that He didn't take advantage of the fact that He was divine. He was doing this in His humanity. What He was showing us was that He's the ultimate Adam, the ultimate human. He was showing us that, like the first Adam in the beginning, He has dominion over all creation, including the (fallen) angels created long before Adam.

What's the point? Jesus had just had a long night. The demands were endless. They'd lined up at the door. The tank was likely empty from the spiritual warfare, and yet, the number one priority when His eyes opened the next morning was not to send a tweet, not to check an email, not to roll over and get more sleep; it was to be present with the Father. In all of the overwhelming busy-ness of life, despite the exhaustion, what mattered most when His eyes opened was presence.

Are you busy? Honestly. The calendar's full. The demands are endless. The issues are piled up at the door...does the busyness of life pull you *away* from the presence of God rather than drive you *to* the presence of God?

Martin Luther once said, "I have so much to do, I shall spend the first three hours in prayer." Now, that sounds like a contradiction, doesn't it? I've got so much to do, I'm going to spend three hours... What? I've got so much to do, I don't have *time* to pray. But Luther's saying the exact opposite, and Jesus is the model. I've got so much to do, I have to be present with God. The point is, if you are busy and tired today, that is all the more reason to withdraw and pray. Fill yourself up with Him, and you will be much more capable to tackle the tasks ahead.

Come to the table and be present with God. Behold His beauty. Think on His glory. Meditate on His truth. Would you come to the table and be present with the Father?

Overburdened was not the only situation in which Jesus pursued intimate presence with the Father. Here's another. Matthew recorded, "*Now when Jesus heard this, he withdrew from there in a boat to a desolate place by himself.*"[79]

What is the context here? Is this the same event as the one related in Mark? Or is this a different occasion in the life of Jesus?

If you go back a few verses, Matthew tells us what Jesus heard that made Him withdraw. "*But when Herod's birthday came, the daughter of Herodias danced before the company and pleased Herod so that he promised with an oath to give her whatever she might ask. Prompted by*

---

79 Matthew 14:13

her mother, she said, 'Give me the head of John the Baptist here on a platter.' And the king was sorry, but because of his oaths and his guests, he commanded it to be given. He sent and had John beheaded in the prison, and his head was brought on a platter and given to the girl, and she brought it to her mother. And his disciples [John's disciples] *came and took the body and buried it. And they went and told Jesus."*

Now we know what Jesus heard. Jesus withdrew and pursued the presence of the Father because He was grieving over the loss of a loved one, namely his cousin. We might think, "But, wait a minute. This is Jesus. He's God after all." You'd think he'd be like, "No big deal. His head got cut off. I'll put it back on." Yeah, I mean, He could say that. He could do that. He's the resurrection and the life, after all. And yet, do you remember His response when He heard of Lazarus's death? What did He do? He said, "Okay, time for a magic show." No, He didn't do that. He ...

Wept.

He wept. He grieved. His heart was broken. When Jesus heard of the death of John the Baptist, He was broken and grieving.

His immediate reflex when His heart was grieving was presence with the Father. Perhaps you have just gone through a loss in your life; lost a loved one to death, or divorce, or long separation. Maybe you're grieving over your empty nest, or a lost job, or a deep hurt. Please listen. If Jesus pursued the presence of the Father in His grief, how much more should we in ours?

If your heart needs healing, go to the Great Physician.

We have a Great Physician, and His office is always open. Make frequent appointments. And continue to make them until your heart is healed. In your grief today, would you come to the table? Would you come to the presence of the Father just as Jesus did in His grief, and would you meditate on His truth, and behold His glory, and think about His beauty, and just be with Him?

Overburdened, grieving. Were those the only occasions when Jesus pursued intimate presence with the Father? No. Here's another, "*In these days, he went out to the mountain to pray and all night he continued in prayer to God.*"[80]

Again, what's the context?

It is given in the very next verse. (By the way, it always helps to read the next verse.)

"*And when day came,*" after He'd been up all night praying, "*he called his disciples and chose from them twelve whom he named apostles.*" Clearly a different occasion. Jesus sought solitude, presence with the Father right before one of the biggest decisions He would make in His ministry: who would be the men who would follow Him, who would journey with Him, who would carry on His work throughout the world?

Now, this is just me speculating, but I wonder if, in that conversation with the Father, Jesus asked, "Peter? Really? *Simon* Peter? The fisherman Peter? And those guys? Surely not them." He probably said that about me,

---

80 Luke 6:12

too. But you can't help but wonder what that conversation was like.

The point is, where did Jesus go right before this major decision? Into the presence of the Father. Are you seeing the humanity of Jesus here? Jesus, whom the Apostle Paul calls "our wisdom" seeks wisdom. Jesus is practicing what the Bible commands us to do. "*If any of you lacks wisdom, let him ask God who gives generously to all without reproach, and it will be given to him.*"[81] And again, in the context of worry and anxiety, "*But seek first the kingdom of God and his righteousness, and all these things will be added to you.*"[82] Before making the important decision of whom He would call to be apostles, His reflex was to be present with the Father.

You may be familiar with the name Hudson Taylor, a very famous missionary who worked in China many years ago. He was exhausted in ministry and went back to England with a major decision weighing heavily on his heart. The decision: does God want me to start a new work in inland China? At that time, most of the work in China was happening in the coastal region. He knew going inland would require a lot of people and money, and it was going to be dangerous. His burning question was, "God, what is your will? What do you want me to do?" Have you ever been there?

In England, he went to visit friends, but rather than enjoying the fellowship of his friends, he took a walk by

---

81 James 1:5
82 Matthew 6:33

himself on the beach. He said that the ocean was peaceful, but his life was not. I'm going to let Hudson tell you what happened. This is the thought the Lord gave him. "If we are obeying the Lord, the responsibility rests on Him, not with us. Thou Lord, thou shalt have all the burden. I'm giving it to You. At Thy bidding, as Thy servant, I go forward leaving the results with Thee." Then he said this. "How restfully I turned away from the sands. The conflict ended and all was at peace. I felt as if I could fly up the hill to Mister Pierce's house, and, oh! how I did sleep that night!"

What happened? Presence. He got alone with God. Struggling with one of the biggest decisions in his ministry, being in God's presence gave him peace.

It's possible that you are in the middle of major decisions in your life. Are you going to marry her? What will you do vocationally? Are you going to make that financial purchase? I encourage you to follow the example of Christ and lean not on your own understanding, but acknowledge Him, pursue Him, go to Him, and He will make your paths straight. Or, I'll say it this way—if your life needs wisdom, then make frequent appointments with the Wonderful Counselor. His office is always open, and you can go to Him any time.

How can you make wise decisions in life if you don't spend time in the presence of wisdom? For wisdom is a Person, not a principle. Would you come to the table? Be present. With all of your distractions in life, be present with the Father.

Overburdened, grieving, making decisions. Are there are any other occasions in our Lord's life when He did this? There is. (There are actually seven specific instances recorded in the New Testament.)

"*And he withdrew from them about a stone's throw and knelt down and prayed.*"[83] Same language that we've seen in all these other verses, and the first question, of course, is what is the context?

The next verse reveals it. "*Saying, 'Father, if you are willing, remove this cup from me. Nevertheless, not my will, but yours be done.' And there appeared to him an angel from heaven strengthening him. And being in agony, he prayed more earnestly, and his sweat became like great drops of blood falling down to the ground.*"

You remember how Jesus struggled with the cup, the wrath of God, and He asked, "Can there be a cross without a cup?" But He surrendered and said, "Not my will. It's your will that I'm here to do."

In suffering, in the darkest night of the soul, in the moment of Jesus' deepest agony, He prayed more earnestly, that is, He sought presence with the Father.

This reminds me of the Psalm:

"As a deer pants for the flowing stream, so pants my soul for you, oh God. My soul thirsts for God, for the Living God. When shall I come and appear before God? My tears have been my food day and night while they say to me all day long 'Where is

---

83 Luke 22:41

*your God?' Why are you cast down, oh my soul?
Why are you in turmoil within me? Hope in God,
for I shall again praise him, my salvation. Deep
calls out to deep. At the roar of your waterfalls,
all your breakers, your waves have gone over me,
but by day the Lord commands his steadfast
love, and at night his song is with me."*

*"A prayer to the God of my life. I say to God, my
rock, why have you forsaken me? Why do I go on
mourning? Because of the oppression of the
enemy. As with a deadly wound in my bones, my
adversaries taunt me while they say to me all day
long, 'Where is your God?' Why are you cast
down, oh my soul? Why are you in turmoil
within me? Hope in God. For I shall again praise
him, my salvation and my God."[84]*

This psalmist, like many others in the Bible and in
church history, went through a normal experience, not a
weak, immature experience, but a normal experience in
the Christian life. A troubled soul, feeling as though God is
absent, asking Him, "God, where are you? It feels like
you've forgotten me. I pray, but I don't hear anything. I
sing, and I don't feel anything. I'm like a deer panting for
water, and I can't get a drop; it's affecting my soul. And the
trials are constant, one thing after another. Wave after
wave keeps crashing on my head, sinking me deeper and

---

84 Psalm 42

deeper down, and I just want to cry out, 'Enough.'" As the hymnist said, "When sorrows like sea billows roll," it affects my soul.

And then, like Job's comforters, others add insult to injury. "Oh, well, God must not care about you, because look at your life. A good Christian would never have to go through something like that." This taunting can affect my thinking. "Maybe this didn't take. Maybe I'm not a Christian. Maybe You don't love me." It is a dark, dark hour.

Yet, the psalmist knew where to go: to the presence of God. "God, my rock, I'm longing for you, oh God. The dark hour of the soul is not pulling me from you. The dark hour of the soul is drawing me to you."

Just like Jesus in the garden.

Are you experiencing the dark hour of the soul? If you're in agony, if you feel bereft and abandoned, pursue His presence until you no longer feel His absence. Your feelings are not reality—He is always there. But He wants you to seek Him. Will you come in? It may be an hour. It may be a month. It may be a year. I don't know how long the season of that dark hour will be, but I do know this, He will break through the dark clouds; but it will never happen until you're present.

Overwhelmed, grieving, making decisions, and in the darkest hour of life. There are more, but you get the pattern, right? This was a consistent pattern in the life of our Savior. He constantly pursued presence with the Father.

What does this mean for us? First, as we look at the humanity of Jesus, we're discovering what it means to actually be human. So, what *does* it mean?

To be human is to be present with God

Why did Jesus do this in His humanity? The answer is because humanity was created to live in the presence of God. Is that not the opening chapters of Genesis, that God created humanity to be with Him and Him with them? Sin took us away from that. Sin isolated us from our Maker. The plan for humanity from the beginning was to be present with God.

Calendars, *iPhones*, *Netflix*, and emails are wonderful human inventions, but they may actually be keeping you from being human. Why? Not only may they be keeping you from being present with other people, but to the degree that you are not being intimately present with God, you are not being fully human, because you were created to be intimately present with Him. We know this to be true, because for all of eternity what will you be? Human, and you will always and forever be present with God. The most human thing you can do is be with God.

Divine connection requires your utmost attention

In a world of distractions, you're going to have to work really hard at this. You're going to have to give it your complete attention.

Tony Reinke wrote, "Attention is the skill of withdrawing from everything to focus on something. It's the opposite of the dizziness of the scatterbrained spectacle-seeker who cannot attend to anything, and that is most of us. We're constantly running around focused on so many things that we don't pay attention to much of anything, particularly the most important thing, which is being present with God.

Jean Fleming wrote, "We live in a noisy, busy world. Silence and solitude seem to fit the era of Victorian lace, high button shoes, and kerosene lamps, rather than an age of television, video games, and headphones. We have become a people with an aversion to quietness and an uneasiness with being alone." That is not an option for us. It's not human.

Charles Spurgeon wrote, "Permit not your minds to be easily distracted, or you will have your devotion destroyed."

Tim Keller wrote, "Imagine you had a lethal condition that you would die from unless you took a specific medicine every night. You miss one night, you die. Would you forget? No. Oh, no. It would be the most crucial thing in your life, and you would never miss." Keller continues, "Well, if we don't pray to God, we're not going to make it."

To the degree that this is not happening, we're not going to make it.

Practically speaking here, what do you *do* when you're at the table? Think on God's Word, sing, write, pray. There's a host of possibilities. We could also talk about how often you do this. Do you take mini retreats during the day, even if it's just a five or 10-minute break?

Is it possible that you might need to have a detox from technology? "What did he just ... Heresy! Take my iPhone away?" I'm not saying there's anything wrong with your iPhone. It's just that it may be keeping you from being human. You may very well need to turn it off and unplug for a while so this can happen.

Maybe we could talk about establishing a place. It appears that Jesus had specific places that He went to frequently just to be alone with God. There are plenty of resources to help you with such questions, to help you develop a habit of spending time with God.

Be aware: this is going to be really hard for several reasons. First, because our culture is all about doing. You'll sit down to spend, let's say, 30 minutes in God's presence thinking on Him, and then you'll get up thinking, "What did I accomplish? Is there anything on my to-do list I can cross off?" See, we're so focused on doing that we don't understand what it means to just *be*.

Secondly, sin is going to make this hard to do, because sin wants to distract and isolate. And we have an enemy who wants anything *but* you spending time with God – especially *alone.*

Lastly, it might be hard because it may be like learning a new language. You may sit there for five minutes and be bored. You may be like, "There's no sound, or color, or anything entertaining. It's like I've been dropped off in China and told, 'Try to communicate,' and I'm frustrated because I don't know how to communicate with a Spirit." But listen. Please. If you will just give it time, it will bear fruit.

I was struck by a passage in Tim Keller's book on prayer. He shares that his prayer life didn't have a breakthrough until later in his life. I was amazed. "Tim Keller?! I thought he came out of the womb praying eight hours a day. I mean ..." Yet he said it took time to cultivate this in his life. But know this: Divine connection is going to require your utmost attention. You may have to crucify your Twitter account, your Facebook, your YouTube, your whatever it is. I don't know what it is in your life, but you must be prepared to crucify those things to be present.

One last point of application: to apply the gospel is to pursue God's presence. The issue of being present with God is at the heart of the gospel, because the fundamental work of Jesus was to create this reality. Jesus came to reconcile us to God. Sin had isolated us, and Jesus came to recreate the reality of intimate communion with God. That was at the very heart of what He came to do.

Think of it. At the incarnation, God became flesh in the person of Jesus Christ, and the name given to him was Emanuel, which means God with us. The whole point of Jesus' coming was God saying, "I want to be with you, and I want you to be with me. I want us to be present."

At the crucifixion, Jesus was separated from the Father so that we can be eternally present with the Father. We can be present with God because Jesus was abandoned by God on the cross. Jesus told the repentant thief next to Him, "Today, you will be with me in paradise."

And the resurrection—in the book of Hebrews we are told that we have a high priest who is alive. He's not like those Old Testament priests who all died. He's alive. He's risen. Do you know what that means? The veil that symbolized the separation between God and humanity is torn open. The office is always ready to make appointments. There is a new and living way by which you can draw near, so *draw near*.

That's the argument of Hebrews. Because of the resurrection, because the tomb was opened, so is the presence of God to you. Meaning that a failure to pursue God's presence is a failure to apply the gospel. If we are not in passionate pursuit of the presence of God, we don't know a thing about the gospel. The very heart of the gospel is that we can enter in.

A very busy but successful businessman came home one night. His seven-year-old son came up to him and said, "Daddy, how much money do you make an hour?" The dad was a little put off by this. "That's none of your business, son." But when he realized that his son was serious, he said, "If you must know, I make $150 an hour." The boy ran out of the room.

A little bit later, the little boy said, "Dad, can I borrow $20?" The dad got irritated. "Did you just ask me how much money I make an hour so that you could bum money off me?" But, again, he realized that his son was serious and beginning to tear up. He said, "I'm sorry. That's not what I meant. Let me ask it a different way. What do you need the money for? And if you need the money for something good, then sure I'll give you $20."

The boy said, "Well, Dad, over the last several months I've been saving up my money, and I've got $130." "$130, son! That's a lot of money! If you've got $130, why do you need 20?" And the child said, "Because then I would have enough to buy an hour of your time."

Are you present? In a world of distractions, are you present? But even more important than being present with family, are you, like your Savior, intimately present with the Father? Because the good news of the gospel is that there is a chair for you, because Jesus died for you. Will you sit down? Will you draw near? I promise you, it will impact your life in ways you cannot even imagine.

It may be that, for the very first time, you'll know what it means to be human.

CHAPTER EIGHT

Fearlessly Honest

"When Jesus had finished speaking, a Pharisee invited Him to eat with Him; so He went in and reclined at the table. But the Pharisee was surprised when he noticed that Jesus did not first wash before the meal. Then the Lord said to him, 'Now then, you Pharisees clean the outside of the cup and of the dish, but inside you are full of greed and wickedness. You foolish people! Did not the one who made the outside make the inside also? But now as for what is inside you— be generous to the poor, and everything will be clean for you. Woe to you, Pharisees, because you

give God a tenth of your mint, rue, and all other kinds of garden herbs, but you neglect justice and the love of God. You should have practiced the latter without leaving the former undone. Woe to you Pharisees, because you love the most important seats in the synagogues and respectful greetings in the marketplaces. Woe to you, because you are like unmarked graves, which people walk over without knowing it.'

"One of the experts in the law [of Moses] answered Him, 'Teacher, when you say these things, you insult us also.' Jesus replied, 'And you experts in the law, woe to you, because you load people down with burdens they can hardly carry, and you yourselves will not lift one finger to help them. Woe to you, because you build tombs for the prophets, and it was your ancestors who killed them. So you testify that you approve of what your ancestors did; they killed the prophets, and you build their tombs.'

"When Jesus went outside, the Pharisees and the teachers of the law began to oppose him fiercely and to besiege him with questions, waiting to catch him in something he might say."[85]

---

85 Luke 11:37-48, 53-54

Many years ago, there was a king. This King had an obsession with one thing, his appearance. He thought of clothes and how he looked constantly. He did not invest his country's resources in their military and security. He did not spend money on entertainment. He did not show concern for the welfare of his people. He spent all of his resources and money expanding his wardrobe. It was said that this king would often change his clothing every hour of the day.

One day, two swindlers came to the king with a plan to take advantage of his obsession and vanity. They offered the king a "once in a lifetime" opportunity. They promised the king the world's greatest clothing. It would be beautiful, made from the finest silk in the world, in beautiful colors. It would be laced with gold stitching. They also told the king that, in addition to beauty and splendor, this clothing would also be magical. They told the king that only those worthy of the king's court would be able to see the magnificent clothing. They told the king he could have the clothing for an enormous price. The king, desperate to have the best clothing in the world, gladly agreed. He spared no expense to immediately pay for the extravagant clothing to be made.

Days passed and the king sent one of his servants to inquire about the progress of the clothing. The servant entered the workshop and immediately noticed that everyone was working very hard, but he could not see what they were working on. But then he remembered that only people worthy of the king's court could see the enchanted clothing. Not wanting to admit that he was unworthy of the king's court, he said nothing. Instead he praised the workers, telling them that the clothing was spectacular. He returned to the king. Hiding his secret, the servant reported to him that the clothing was beautiful and perfect for such a noble king.

Several days later the king sent another servant to check on the progress of his investment. This servant traveled to the workshop and saw everyone diligently working, though, like the previous servant, he could not see any actual clothing. But he, too, remembered that the creators of the magical clothing had declared that only those worthy of the king's court would see the elegant clothing. Desperate to prove that he was worthy, the servant applauded the workers on their progress. When he returned to the king he shared nothing but praise for the new clothing.

The day finally came when the clothing was ready and, with great pomp, was delivered to the king. Excitedly, the king opened the box and, to his dismay, saw nothing. It looked like an empty box. Remembering the words of the gentleman who sold him the clothing, he realized that he could not see the clothing because he was not worthy to be king. Ashamed and frightened that the people of his court would believe that he was a fraud and not the rightful king, he said nothing. The king strip off his clothes and puts on his new clothes.

All the people in his court praised him, telling him how wonderful he looked in his magnificent clothing. Praise upon praise, they continued to flatter him. Puffed up with pride and flattery, the king decided to parade down the streets of his kingdom so that all the people of the land could give him praise. The parade continued, until one wise little boy declared, for all to hear, "The emperor has no clothes!" And yet the crowd, for fear of what the king might do, and the king, for fear of what the crowd might think, said nothing. The truth was never spoken.

Hans Christian Anderson made this tale, "The Emperor's New Clothes," famous. It was a story written for children, but also is a very telling parable for adults. Every single one of us has been in situations where we knew there was a problem and should have spoken up. We should have said something. But, instead, we pretended like nothing was wrong. We have all been there. We have noticed that a friend had lettuce in his teeth, or something hanging from his nose…yet we said nothing. We did not want to do the uncomfortable. We did not want to make things awkward.

Or we had a coworker who wasn't performing. Because we disliked conflict we weren't honest about that employee's performance, and we softened the review. Perhaps it was our child who was out of control. We preferred to be his friend rather than his parent, because consistently confronting and dealing with issues is difficult. Or when we hear someone criticize or question Christianity and we remain silent. After all, we want to fit in.

Maybe when your spouse asks, "Does this make me fat?" you say nothing. This actually shows wisdom. :)

The point is that being honest about certain things is a difficult thing for us to do sometimes, whether it is being honest with a person, God, or ourselves. Much of the time it is easier to simply go with the flow and praise the emperor's clothes than address the real problem. So, we need to ask ourselves, "Am I the type of person that speaks the truth when the truth needs to be spoken?"

This does not mean we always have to give our opinion on everything to every person with whom we interact. We are not called to be "Jerks for Jesus." In fact, *how* we address something is just as important as what we say. Sometimes a wise person must choose to hold his or her tongue. We need to speak the truth with wisdom and grace.

Are we the kind of people that, in love, speak the truth when the truth needs to be spoken? This fearless honesty is what we see in our Savior in Luke's gospel. "*When Jesus had finished speaking, a Pharisee asked Him to dine with him, so Jesus went and reclined at the table.*" Jesus was invited for lunch at the home of a Pharisee.

There are two important things to note so that we understand the significance. First, in Jesus' culture, sharing a meal was a significant event. To dine with someone was not a casual thing. It was important. It was relational. It was a sign of intimacy. Jesus, throughout His ministry, shared meals with many different kinds of people. He ate with tax collectors and sinners. If I could relate it to today's world, during these meals Jesus had some wings and Pabst Blue ribbon, listened to Lynyrd Skynyrd, talked about everything from sports to the real and difficult issues of life. He also ate with the religious people. These meals were filled with discussion of the authenticity and accuracy of various versions of the Bible, with everyone dressed in their Sunday best. Chris Tomlin was playing in the background as they debated the cultural relevance of head coverings, instead of the real issues of life. They pretended that life was perfect.

Jesus ate with both types of sinners, the religious kind and the irreligious kind. This is good news for us because it shows that the grace of God extends to all. Sharing a meal had significance.

Second, the Pharisee was significant. Pharisees have a very negative connotation in today's Christianity. We see them as bad. But in the time of Jesus, that would not have been the case. They were the ruling, religious, political class in Israel. They were loved and respected by the people. They were educated leaders. They were popular. They were morally upright people. And they took great pride in their prestige and moral superiority.

They created rules. They created traditions. They equated these rules and traditions with scripture, and used them to separate themselves from everyone else. The very name, Pharisee, means separate one. They elevated themselves above others by submitting to their man-made rules. "*The Pharisee was astonished to see that Jesus did not first wash before dinner.*" Washing of the hands when a person came home was one of the traditions that the Pharisees had created and then implemented as if it were a command of God.

Now, this may not seem like a huge deal. In the age of germs and hand sanitizer this seems acceptable. In fact, in those days it may have been common sense to clean yourself when you returned home for a meal. It's just good personal hygiene, right?

But for the Pharisees it was not a matter of personal hygiene. It was smug self-righteousness. They washed their hands when they returned home to wash off any chance of contact with a Gentile. They did not want to risk that a part of the outside world, a door knob, a cup, anything they may have touched had been touched by someone who was unclean. So they would purify themselves, so that they could then tell the world how clean they were, and look down on those who did not take these extra steps for purity.

Knowing this to be true about the Pharisee, what did Jesus do? He walked past the water basin and went straight to the table, seemingly not caring if he "defiled" anything in the Pharisee's home. It was the equivalent today to someone coming to our home for dinner, sitting at the table and sticking his dirty fingers directly into the bowl of potato salad. We would not be pleased with this. The Pharisees reaction to Jesus was the same. They were in disbelief. They were offended. Their lives had been given over to the belief that cleanliness is next to Godliness. Imagine you invited a guest to your house. When he entered your home he refused to take off his shoes, he tracked dirt all over the floor, he ate before everyone else had been served, he used his hands instead of the provided silverware, and he double dipped in the guacamole. Sounds awful, right? Blatant disrespect! This is how the Pharisees felt.

So how did Jesus respond? *"The Lord said to him, 'Now you Pharisees cleanse the outside of the cup and of the dish, but inside you're full of greed and wickedness. You fools. Did not He who made the outside make the inside also, but give alms those there within and behold everything is clean, for you that is what matters is the heart, what matters is the inside. But woe to you, the Pharisees, for you love the best seat in the synagogues. You love the greetings in the marketplaces. Woe to you, for you are like unmarked graves and people walk over them without knowing it.'"*

Jesus certainly did not hold back. Jesus responded to their self-righteous piety by calling them greedy, wicked hypocrites that only cared about social status and physical appearance. He told them that, in reality, on the inside they were dead, even like an unmarked grave that no one can see. Can you even imagine how awkward this was? How uncomfortable?

Jesus was willing to tell the emperor that he was not wearing clothes. He was willing to say what no one else would say. He spoke the truth.

Then someone responded to Jesus. *"One of the experts in the law* [of Moses] *answered Him, 'Teacher, when you say these things, you insult us also.'* In other words Jesus hurt their feelings. Jesus hurt their self esteem. *"Jesus replied, 'And you experts in the law, woe to you, because you load people down with burdens they can hardly carry, and you yourselves will not lift one finger to help them. Woe to you, because you build tombs for the prophets, and it was your ancestors who killed them. So you testify that you approve of what your ancestors did; they killed the prophets, and you build their tombs."*

Wow. Jesus was an equal opportunity offender. He made sure that everyone in the room was offended before the conversation was over. This seems so unlike the meek, compassionate, gracious and forgiving Jesus that we see throughout most of His ministry. It makes us uncomfortable. But one of the things we need to realize is that while Jesus is loving, gracious, comforting, and forgiving, our Savior does have other sides. We must expose and learn from the sides that we do not typically want to talk about. We often want to keep Jesus in the box of the sweet and mild man who welcomed little children. We do not know how to react to this Jesus who says the emperor has no clothes.

Jesus was simply being honest. In His humanity as a prophet, He was discerning, as He often did, the heart and intentions of the Pharisees. He saw beyond the outward appearance and looked at the motives. This is an important implication. There is a difference between being offensive and saying something that offends. In our world today people take offense to many things. The offender is labeled as hateful, judgmental or intolerant. Sometimes this is true. But truly being offensive is different than saying something that may offend.

For example, a racial slur reveals the ugly in the person who says it. Exposing a friend's drinking problem actually can be an act of love, and it reveals the brokenness in the friend. It is not meant to offend, even if the friend takes offense. In this light, Jesus' words are not offensive, but it was what was inside the Pharisee's heart that was offensive. Jesus simply brought it to light. He exposed it for what it truly was. He spoke the truth. He addressed the reality of their hearts.

Knowing and understanding this we may still ask, "But why does Jesus have to be so aggressive?" It is so unlike the attitude and characteristics He shows elsewhere in scripture. He did not call the Samaritan woman names for having five husbands. So why did Jesus choose this particular moment to be so fearlessly honest? Why was he brutal in His honesty? There are three reasons why Jesus chose to be fearlessly honest.

First, Jesus was fearlessly honest with the Pharisees because of the degree of their depravity. In other words, Jesus spoke this way to the Pharisees because of a quality that they had that was not found in others to whom Jesus ministered. They had hardened hearts. For Jesus, the harder the heart, the harder the language that He used. Jesus did not speak this way to those who were broken. To those who were hurting. To those who were humble sinners. Jesus spoke this way to people who were hardened. This is very important. This does not mean that Jesus was any less honest with others. His approach, however, was vastly different. Jesus did expose the Samaritan woman's sinful past, but He did not do it aggressively. This is because the heart of the recipient was opened, was soft, was seeking truth.

Imagine a piece of fruit, such as cantaloupe, we know that it has a tough rind. But the inside is fairly soft. So we can take something heavy, such as a mallet, and if we strike it we will begin to leave indents, or impressions. We do not have to hit it very hard to leave an impression. It does not take that much. However, some objects, such as a brick, are hard throughout. A soft strike with a mallet or hammer will do nothing to a brick. Not a dent, not a scratch, nothing at all. Our hearts are either soft, like the cantaloupe, or hard like a brick. When our hearts are soft, a soft and gentle word of truth will suffice to pierce the heart. But with a hard heart, more force may be needed to get the truth to break through.

We must be honest with ourselves. Sometimes our hearts are so hard that we need brutally honest words to break our hearts. We become callous and hardened for many different reasons, in many different areas of our lives. This is why Jesus speaks hard words to us. He wants to break our hearts. He wants to break through and deal with the real issues in our lives, but He knows that in order to do so we will have to face some harsh truths.

The second reason that Jesus chose to be fearlessly honest was because of the nature of His ministry. Since Jesus came to call the hearts of people to return to God, He did this by getting to the heart of the issue at hand. This is why He refused to play religious games with the Pharisees. He did not engage in superficial talk. He did not dodge hard topics because it was awkward or uncomfortable. His purpose was to get to the heart of the issue. The motives behind the actions. The agenda behind the practices. The spirit behind the law.

Jesus wants to cleanse the heart. The Pharisees cared more about cleaning the outside than the inside. They cared about the external. They were like the emperor, finding worth and identity in their "new clothes." In their appearance to others. In their standing in the community. In their superficial self-righteousness. But Jesus went after their hearts, confronting them with what was really important.

There are many examples of this in the ministry of Jesus. When the rich young ruler came to Jesus, he bragged to Jesus by telling Him that he kept all the commandments. He knew he looked good on the outside. But Luke related, "*When Jesus heard this, He said to him, 'One thing you still lack. Sell all that you have and distribute to the poor and you will have treasure in Heaven and come follow me.' But when he heard these things, he became very sad, for he was extremely rich.*"[86]

What did Jesus do? He stripped him bare. He asked the rich young ruler to give up all the superficiality of his life to follow him. He got to the real issue.

Another example is found in the story of Mary and Martha. Martha told Jesus to chastise Mary for sitting at Jesus' feet instead of working hard in the kitchen like Martha was doing. She told Jesus to tell Mary to stop worshiping Him in order to take care of the busy work. "*The Lord answered her, Martha, Martha. You are anxious*

---

86 Luke 18:22

and troubled about many things. But one thing is necessary. Mary has chosen the good portion which will not be taken away from her."[87]

What did Jesus do? He stripped her bare. He tells her that worshiping at Jesus' feet is more important than the busy tasks of the home. He dealt with her heart and the real issues of her life.

After the crowds had eaten their fill and were, therefore, following Jesus, John says that Jesus told them, *"Truly, truly I say to you, you're seeking me not because you saw signs, but because you ate your fill of loaves."*[88] Jesus got to the real issue.

The disciples had high hopes of what a life of ministry would look like. But Jesus got to the real issue and told them, *"Behold, I am sending you out as sheep in the midst of wolves. Beware of men. For they will deliver you over to courts and flog you in their synagogues and you will be dragged before governors and kings for my sake to bear witness before them and the Gentiles."*[89] Not exactly a motivational speech. He spoke the truth. He got to the heart of the issue of what it would mean to follow Him.

Mark recorded a story about a fig tree. The tree was bare, and Jesus was hungry. *"And seeing in the distance a fig tree in leaf, He went to see if He could find anything on it, and when He came to it He found nothing but leaves, for it was not the season for fig. And Jesus said to it, 'May*

87 Luke 10:41
88 John 6:26
89 Matthew 10:16

no one ever eat fruit from you again.'"[90] Ok, that story does not fit with the rest, but I think it is hilarious.

To Peter, Jesus said, "Get thee behind me, Satan!"

To the Pharisees He said, "You're of your father the devil."

To Nicodemus, He said, "You're a teacher and you don't know these things."

To the one who wanted security, He said, "The son of man has no place to lay his head."

And to every single one of us who thinks we will enter the kingdom on our own, He says, "I am the Way, I am the Truth, and I am the Life. No one gets to the Father except through me."

So, what is the point? The point is that Jesus spent the bulk of His ministry telling people they have no clothes. The very nature of His ministry was to get to the heart of the issue, because He was always after the heart of the person. The very nature of His ministry demanded that He speak with fearless honesty.

The third reason why Jesus was so fearlessly honest is that He came for the restoration of real humanity. As we have already learned, Jesus was the ultimate human. He was and is the ultimate Adam. So in His life on earth He showed us what real humanity looks like. We do not want to admit that our experience is subhuman, or not fully human the way God intended it to be. Jesus came so that He could provide a way to take us back to how God created us to be. He cleansed the temple to show that we were

90 Mark 11:13

created to worship God. He raised Lazarus from the dead because we were created to live. He fed the 5000 because we were created to eat under the provision of God, like in the garden. Jesus was tempted because we were created to live in victory over sin. Humanity was not created to sin.

So how does Jesus' honesty take us back to true humanity? Here is the answer. Humanity was created to live in an open, honest relationship with God and other people. It was not until sin came into the world that Adam and Eve put clothes" on.

When sin came in, we started hiding. It is why the Pharisees, in Luke's gospel, were doing what mankind had been doing ever since Genesis 3. They were covering up. They used prestige, traditions, practices and self-righteousness to hide who they really were. They had to cover up the ugliness of their hearts.

In the movie, The Wizard of Oz, the wizard says, "Pay no attention to the man behind the curtain." He did not want to be exposed for the fraud that he was. So Jesus speaks fearlessly honestly, to expose us. Why? Not just to expose us and leave us there, but to take us back to God. We were not created to hide from God. We were created to live in a free-flowing, honest fellowship with God. And not just with God, but with one another, in community.

In the beginning, the emperor had no clothes, and God said that it was good. In the beginning, there was nothing to be ashamed of. In the beginning, humanity was free to be who we were. In the beginning, there was no need to hide. Sin made us run. Sin made us cover up. And we have been hiding in the bushes ever since. Jesus speaks the truth because He wants to take us back to what we were created for. That is the reason for His fearless honesty.

So how do we, ourselves, experience Jesus' honesty? We have seen examples of it. We understand the reason for it. But how can we actually experience it in our own lives? How do we take what we have learned and apply to our everyday lives the honesty of Jesus speaking into us the way He spoke into the lives of the Pharisees?

First, we must let the truth of Christ that is Scripture speak into our lives. "*For the word of God is living and active. It is sharper than any two edged sword. It pierces to the division of soul and spirit, joints and marrow, the discerning of the thoughts and intentions of the heart. No creature is hidden*" [that is Genesis language] "*from His sight, but all are naked and exposed.*"[91] When we read scripture we are naked and exposed, hungry to be filled with the knowledge of what God wants from us. The Word exposes who we are to the eyes of Him to whom we must give account. We have got to understand this. God helps us to see this. The Word of God is taking us back. It is restoring us.

Paul tells us, "*All Scripture is breathed out by God, it is profitable for teaching, for reproof, for correction, for training in righteousness.*"[92] If we do not embrace the conviction of Scripture, we will soon become calloused, possibly hindering our growth. We instead need to come

91 Hebrews 4:12
92 2 Timothy 3:16

to a place where we are soft, not hardened, with each other. We must declare that we are sinners in need of a gracious Jesus, who is ready to meet us where we are and heal our sin. There is a Savior. And we find Him in the Word of God.

We must proclaim the Word of Christ, because it is in the Word that Christ speaks honesty into our lives and begins to take us back to what we were created to be. The gospel can be harsh. It can be gentle. The gospel will bring us to our knees and then lift us up with grace. We need both if we are going to be conformed into the image of Christ. Let the Word of Christ, Scripture, speak into your life.

Second, speak the truth of Christ into other people's lives. Not harshly for the sake of argument. Not being a jerk. But simply speaking the truth in love. This is difficult for many people. Some of us have non-confrontational personalities. But if we are not willing to speak truth when prompted by our relationship with Christ, then we are not loving others the way Christ loves us. How can we say we love the truth and we love others if we are not willing to share it? To really love others, we MUST speak the truth. Even when it is uncomfortable. Even when it is awkward. Even when the recipient takes offense.

One author says this, "We chit-chat. We spend our days at a level of conversation that is as substantial as smoke. We dance around one another like birds in a mating ritual, bobbing, ducking, puffing out our chest, flapping our wings and circling one another."

We must be honest. It is not necessarily our natural tendency, because people who are honest sometimes get hurt. Sometimes there is backlash. Can you imagine telling your mother-in-law that she is controlling? Or telling a friend he is self-centered? We hold back the truth because we fool ourselves thinking that we love them too much to hurt their feelings. But the reality is, we care about them too little. We selfishly say nothing because we fear tension, backlash, penalties, or rejection. We would rather allow them to remain a hardened Pharisee than speak honestly. We default to the easy, wide path where it is a lot more comfortable to simply praise the emperor's clothing than to tell him that we know what is showing.

God has given us the body of Christ to speak the word of Christ into one another's lives. This should be a wake-up call for us. Parents, friends, husbands, wives, in this culture there will be seasons when we will not be popular. We may be like the little boy in the crowd who bravely says, "The emperor has no clothes."

This does not give us permission to go on a verbal rampage and be brutally honest at our whim to anyone that crosses us. We do not have the right to berate or verbally attack another person. Our motive must always be the love of Christ. The Holy Spirit helps us to present the truth in the most effective way if we listen to Him.

"*Better is open rebuke than hidden love. Faithful are the wounds of a friend, profuse are the kisses of an enemy.*"[93] A true friend will wound when necessary,

---

93 Proverbs 27:5-6

because they are faithful. The Hebrew word is that of giving support, upholding, nourishing. We often pay therapists to speak truth into our lives. There is nothing wrong with this. And I'm not saying to fire your therapist. If we have good friends, and we are being good friends, we should be doing the same thing. We should be willing to speak fearlessly honest truth into each other's lives. In contrast, an enemy, or a friend with bad motives, praises when he should rebuke. Yet that is often the type of relationship we want. We just want to hear how good our "new clothes" look. We do not want to actually hear the convicting truth. When we find a good friend who speaks truth, we need to learn not to take offense. We don't need to change friends, we need to change our lives.

We will become like the Pharisees when we desire the honor of people more than the honesty of Jesus. We often are not as honest as we should be. We often act just like that emperor. We try on a new outfit every hour of the day just to keep up an appearance. Or we know the truth, but lack the courage or desire to say it, because we want to stay comfortable. To the degree that either of these are true in our lives, is the level in which we are not applying the gospel to our lives.

After all, do you remember what happened 2000 years ago to a real king? He was taken out into the streets and put before others. "*The soldiers took Jesus into the governors headquarters and they gathered the whole*

[94]battalion before Him and they stripped Him of His clothes."

Don't you see? Jesus was stripped of His clothes so that we could be naked and unashamed before God as we were created to be. Jesus was stripped of His clothes so that we would stop hiding under man-made religion and moralistic fig leaves. The good news of the gospel is that the real emperor wore no clothes so that we could be clothed in His righteousness. So we can stop trying to wash the dirt off of our hands and, instead, let Jesus purify our hearts. When that happens we will see God.

---

94 Matthew 27:27

CHAPTER NINE

Selflessly Humble

"Now before the feast of the Passover, when Jesus knew that the hour had come to depart out of this world to the father, having loved his own who were in the world, he loved them to the end. During supper, when the devil had already put it into the heart of Judas Iscariot, Simon's son, to betray him, Jesus, knowing that the father had given all things into his hands, and that he had come from God and was going back to God, rose from supper. He laid aside his outer garments, and taking a towel, he tied it around his waist. Then he poured water into a basin and began to

wash the disciples' feet and to wipe them with the towel that was wrapped around him. He came to Simon Peter who said to him, "Lord, do you wash my feet?" Jesus answered him, "What I'm doing, you do not understand now. But afterward, you will understand." Peter said to him, "You shall never wash my feet." Jesus answered him, "If I do not wash you, you have no share with me." Simon Peter said to him, "Lord, not my feet only, but also my hands and my head." Jesus said to him, "The one who is bathed does not need to wash except for his feet, but is completely clean. And you are clean, but not every one of you." For he knew who was to betray him; that was why he said, "Not all of you are clean."[95]

He was one of the most famous and heroic kings to ever sit on the throne in Scotland. You've probably heard the name if you've ever seen the movie Braveheart. I'm not referring to William Wallace, I'm referring to the King, Robert the Bruce. He was king in Scotland during the 14th century. There are a lot of stories about his life, but there's one story that may be the most famous of all.

The Bruce had conquered a lot of lands, he had traveled to a lot of different places. But there was one place that he'd never been and that was the Holy Land. He

---

95 John 13:1-11

made a vow to God that he would make a pilgrimage to the Holy Land, but then he had a stroke. He knew he would not be able to fulfill that vow that he had made to God.

So he made a rather odd final request. He asked that, after his death, his heart would be removed from his body and that one of his knights would take it to the Holy Land. The knight who volunteered for that mission was a man by the name of James Douglas, a very dear friend to the Bruce.

As was promised, when Robert died they took the heart out of his body and they placed it into a little container that they literally hung around Douglas's neck. And he set off for the Holy Land.

Douglas fought battle after battle as he traveled on this mission, carrying the heart of his king around his neck at all times. Then, in 1330, in yet another battle, he was surrounded and unable to escape. The story goes that he tore that heart from around his neck and threw it into the enemy lines shouting this, "Fight for the heart of your king. Forward, brave heart, as ever thou were wont to do, and Douglas will follow his king's heart or die."

And die Douglas did, and his body was returned to Scotland. I tell you that story, not because I want to interest you with some cool Scottish history. My intent is not even to motivate you to some kind of personal bravery. I share that story because there's something in it I want you to think about.

If you are a follower of Jesus Christ, I have a question for you. Christian, when you go out into the world, do you take the heart of your King with you? When you go to the office in the morning, when you interact with your neighbor next door, when you have that conversation with your spouse, when you interact with other people online, do you carry the heart of your King with you?

Because the truth of the matter is, if you're a Christian, that Jesus has called you out of the world, and then sent you back into the world in order to display Him in the world. You've been called out, and sent in, to display Jesus to the world. What does that look like?

Jesus shows us in John exactly what that looks like. This is a passage with which you are probably familiar, and because of that, it's easy to jump into the story and miss the obvious. So let's take a step back and see the big picture, and then we'll unpack the event itself.

Jesus said, "*For I have given you an example that you also should do just as I have done to you.*"[96] So the purpose of this is for you to do it. More on that in a moment. "*Truly, truly I say to you, whoever receives the one I send receives me, and whoever receives me receives the one who sent me.*"[97]

Jesus was saying, "This is what I expect from my representatives in the world. As you go into the world, as I send you out, this is how I want you to live. This is what I want you to do." In other words, when you look at this side of the savior, you need to realize it's a side of the Savior intended to be reflected in you.

---

96 John 13:15
97 John 24:20

Or we might ask it this way: what do I see in Jesus, here in this passage, that the world should see in me? That's what we should be asking, because Jesus wants us to do this as we are sent out. So, let's see what Jesus wants. "*Before the Feast of the Passover, when Jesus knew that his hour had come to depart out of this world to the father, having loved his own who were in the world, he loved them to the end.*"

The first very obvious thing we see in this passage is the love that Jesus had for His disciples. John was basically giving you a summary statement as to what defined Jesus' ministry as it related to His own. Loving His own to the end implies that what He was doing here was a display of His love.

John was saying, "Jesus's life was defined by his unconditional, sacrificial love for his own." Let me ask a few questions. Why did Jesus love the disciples? Well, it's because they were expert fishermen. Intellectual scholars, right? I mean, these men were incredible. Their resumes: impeccable. They had great insights into Messianic prophecy, right?

Of course not. Jesus loved them...because He loved them. This is important for us to understand about the love of Jesus. Jesus' love was not based on their giftedness, it was based on His grace. It always is. "*While we all once lived in the passions of our flesh, carrying out the desires of the body and the mind, and we were by nature children of wrath like the rest of mankind, but God, being rich in mercy because of the great love with which he loved*" *us...*"[98] The answer to the question of why God loves us is this, because He just does.

He's rich in mercy. He's abounding in love. Trust me, you do not want the love of God to be based on you. We do not want God's love to be based on condition. We don't want God's love to be based on *us*. We want God's love to be based on *Him*, and the good news of the gospel is, it is. He loves you not based on your giftedness, but because of His grace. That is why Jesus loved His disciples. How did He love them? Extravagantly, abundantly.

John said, "The word became human." Paul told the Philippians, "He didn't stop at being human, Jesus went all the way to the point of a slave. Then He didn't stop at being a slave, he went all the way to death on the cross." "He's the bread," John said, "that doesn't just fill your stomach but gives you the reality of never hungering again for anything else. He's the Good Shepherd that doesn't just lead in wisdom and fight in power, He lays down his life for His sheep." In other words, when you really think about the love of Jesus, it goes far beyond any love you can possibly comprehend.

Behold the heart of your King. What defines this Savior is an amazing love, and it's not just a love that He had for His disciples, it's a love that He has for you. I hope that this will go deep into your heart. If you're His, if you belong to Him, Jesus loves you. In fact, He loved you *before* you were His. He doesn't love you because you're a great asset. He doesn't love you because you're more holy

---

98 Ephesians 2:3

than anybody else in the room, because you're rich, because you're attractive, because you're American.

It has nothing to do with your giftedness. It has everything to do with His grace. He doesn't love you because you first loved Him. He loves you because, well, He loves you. He has loved you from the beginning. He loves you right this very moment. He will love you to the end. Behold the heart of your King. And you say, "No chance. You don't know what I've done. You don't know who I am. You don't know what I have in my past." Okay, let me ask you this. Have you ever, in your past, personally sought out the death of Christians? No? Or even, yes?

Let me tell you about a guy who did. His name was Paul. He wanted Christians dead. Then Jesus got hold of him. Listen to what Paul said in a letter to the Galatian church, "I have been crucified with Christ. It's no longer I who live, but it's Christ who lives in me. The life I now live in the flesh, I live by faith in the Son of God, who loved me and gave himself for me."[99]

Oh, see the love of Jesus for you. We can't stop there, though. He not only loves us, but He loves us that we might display that love in the world. Look just a few verses later, "A new commandment I give you: Love one another. As I have loved you, so you must love one another. By this, everyone will know that you are my disciples, if you love one another."[100]

---

99 Galatians 2:20
100 John 13:34

In other words, I'm sending you out, and they'll know you're Mine, how? Because you love one another as I have loved you. In other words, when you go out into the world, make sure you take the heart of your King with you. But how does that get expressed? He shows us in our primary text. "*During supper knowing that the Father had given all things into His hands, and that He had come from God, and was going back to God, Jesus rose from supper. He laid aside His outer garments,* [just as He had laid aside His divine rights and attributes], *tied a towel around his waist, poured water into a basin, and began to wash and dry His disciples' feet.*" He performed the work of the lowliest servant.

Luke helps give us some context as to what's happening in this moment, because Luke informs us that, at this time, the disciples were fighting over who was the greatest. Who gets shotgun in the Jesus van, that's what they want to know. Who gets the best seat at the table? The context here is that the disciples are talking smack at this very meal. They are consumed with themselves. They want to know, "What's in it for me? What will I get out of this?" It is in that context that Jesus does something scandalous.

Because you may be familiar with this passage, it may not catch you like it ought to catch you. This is a scandal. What Jesus does, no one does. This is humiliating. It is unbelievable and unthinkable. I'm not going to spend much time here on the foot washing itself in terms of what's at stake here. I'm going to talk more about Jesus. But let me just say a few things about foot washing. First of all, it was necessary in those days. It's still necessary today. If your feet stink, wash them. That might be the best application you get today, I don't know. It was quite necessary in those days because, as you know, they were walking almost everywhere they went in sandals, open shoes, stepping in dirt, mud, animal waste, and more.

Of all the parts of the body, the most disgusting part, because of their culture, was their feet. That made foot washing not just necessary, but unbelievably nasty. They didn't take care of their feet the way many people do today. Feet were absolutely filthy, which is why the job of foot-washing was humiliating. Jewish rabbis would not even let Jewish servants do this. If you had a Gentile slave or servant, that was fine, you could make them do it. But not a Jew. If you had any status at all, no chance. I'm trying to get into your mind: This isn't done. That is why Peter pushed back, "You're not washing my feet. There is no way I'm going to let you do that."

So in this action of Jesus washing the feet of his disciples, we see incredible humility. I'm just going to point out five things.

Jesus got low, though His status was high

Remember that they were partaking of the Passover meal, they were celebrating the Passover. Who, by His own admission, said that He was the fulfillment of the Passover? Jesus. "This is my body. This is my blood."

Jesus was saying, "Everything that you've been celebrating about the Passover has always been pointing to me. It is fulfilled in me." In other words, no one had a higher status as that table than Jesus. As John said, He's the eternal word, the light of the world, the bread of life, the good shepherd, the resurrection and the life, and the One who gives living water. Yet, here we see Jesus sticking his Messianic fingers into the nasty toes of common fishermen. We see the One with the greatest status in the room take the lowest position in the room.

Let your mind dwell on this. Had you been in the room, He would have washed *your* dirty feet. Now you think about that. Imagine Jesus taking off your shoes, looking at your feet, and the eternal King of all creation washing your feet. I have no problem understanding why I should be at the feet of Jesus. I can't imagine Jesus at mine. That's why I don't blame Peter, because I'd have reacted the same way. There's no way that the person of highest status should go this low, and yet, behold the heart of your King. The One with the highest status in the room took the lowest place in the room.

Jesus got low, though his death was eminent

If you know your timeline, you know that Jesus died the next day. Do you think you'd be distracted? Do you think you'd have a few things on your mind? For goodness sake, I get more distracted the closer I get to my weekend sermon. By Thursday or Friday, my kids come up to me and I'm like, "I don't even know who you are. You look familiar." Because the closer it gets to the weekend, the more my mind is focused on that. In other words, Jesus was able to block out the circumstances of the time, the deadly serious circumstances, and focus on serving His disciples.

This is so important. Jesus didn't let the circumstances of his life get in the way of serving those in His life. It would have been easy to say, "You know what guys, not now. I'm just not up to it. I know what's coming tomorrow. A little bit of a downer. If you'd just excuse me, I think I'm not going to do this." And yet, even with all of the weighty stuff that was happening, he got low.

Jesus got low though His betrayer was in the room

His betrayer was present. "*During supper when the devil had already put into the heart of Judas Iscariot, Simon's son, to betray him...*" I mean, it's one thing to wash the feet of your friends, it's an entirely different thing to do it to one who is actively working against you—to your death. I mean, if this were me, I'd be like, "No chance. I heard what you said about my sermon. There's no way I'm washing *your* feet."

We all experience conflict with people. We all have people that we don't get along with. But look at the humility of Jesus. It blows my mind to think that the very one who was planning to betray Jesus with a kiss got his feet washed. Behold the heart of your King.

Paul agreed, "*For one will scarcely die for a righteous person, perhaps for a good person one would dare even to die...*"[101] But here's what makes His love so amazing. God shows His love for us because *while we were still sinners*, Paul even calls us enemies, *Christ died for us*. The truth is, you're the betrayer in the room and so am I. And He would still wash our feet.

This is a passage that really helps us understand the difference between Christianity and Satanism. Wait, what? "Did he say, Satan?" This is so clear. You see right before you what Christianity is about, and what Satanism is about. The text says the devil put betrayal into Judas's heart. So, Satan was present there. Here's what you need to understand, Satanism is not killing chickens, drinking blood, and getting 666 tattoos on your forehead. That's not Satanism. Satanism is this: it's self-exaltation.

That's why Satan fell, because he wanted to exalt himself to God-status. That's exactly what he tempted Adam and Eve with in the garden. Why be under God when you could be your own God? Satanism, from the very beginning, has been self-exaltation, which is why when it says that the devil put this in his heart, it might mean more, but it at least means this, Judas got selfish. Because all it takes to be a Satanist is to be consumed with yourself. If you don't believe me, go back to John 8. Jesus looked at the Pharisees and all their spiritual arrogance, and do you know what He said? "*You are just like your father, the devil.*"

---

101 Romans 5:7

He was not saying, "You know, I see horns coming out of your head. That resembles somebody." He was saying, "That arrogant heart is not new. It goes back a really long time." You want to be a Satanist, all you have to do is live for yourself. You want to follow Jesus, you're going to serve even the enemy in the room. He got low.

He got low and wanted nothing in return

"When he had washed their feet and put on his outer garments and resumed his place, he said to them, 'Do you understand what I have done to you? You call me Teacher and Lord, and you're right. So I am. If I then, your Lord and Teacher, have washed your feet, you also ought to wash one another's feet.'" Now that's not how you would expect that to go. We would expect it to go like this, "Now that I have washed your feet, you wash mine. I am, after all, your Lord and Teacher. That's how it works. I have washed your feet, and now you wash mine."

But that's not what Jesus said. Jesus had no interest in having His feet washed. He makes very clear that He came to serve, not to be served. Please get this. A humble servant gets so lost in serving, he loses all self-interest. He's not concerned about himself, he's concerned about the good of the other. You might say, "Yeah, but aren't we supposed to serve God?" Yes, and you serve God by serving others. That's what Jesus was saying, because God doesn't need anything. You're not bringing God something that He doesn't already own.

Yes, you serve God, and how do you serve God? By serving one another. Perhaps you have loved, you have served, and you have gotten nothing in return. You've felt forgotten and gotten upset. "How hard I work for this family. Do you know what I've done for this church?" To you I say, behold the heart of your King.

Jesus got low when no one else would

Where do I get this idea? Two places in the text: "During supper…" and "Jesus arose during supper…." Now, why is that important? Because historically and traditionally, we know something. And it rhymes, too, so it's going to be easy to remember. In those days, they would wash their feet before they'd eat, just like your mama told you, right? Did your mom ever tell you that? "Wash your feet before you eat." Okay, maybe not, but that was true in those days.

The reason it was the case was because their feet weren't underneath a table like they are for us in our day. They would recline at table. What that means is that somebody else's feet would be right out there in your face, not decently hidden away. And you're trying to eat. "Peter! Like, what'd you step in, bro? Oh, you got some nasty toe fungus, dude. Get something on that. I'm trying to eat bread here."

The whole point is, because that's the way they would recline at the table, you would wash your feet before you eat. The reason why this hadn't already been done was because nobody was willing to do it. It should have already happened, but it hadn't because they were too consumed with arguing about who was the greatest. So, Jesus got up during supper and he washed their feet. Jesus did what no one else was willing to do.

You know that's true in many ways, isn't it? He has done what no one else would ever do. Look at the lowliness of Jesus here. And remember that He is setting us an example, "I'm sending you out into the world, and this is how I want you to live. I want you to love the way I've loved you, and I want you to serve the way I've served you." In other words, when you go out into the world, make sure you take the heart of your King with you.

There is one more piece of this passage that must be mentioned. This text is pointing us to something much greater than washing feet. In fact, the entire scenario is really not even about washing feet, it's about something else Jesus had come to do. "*Jesus answered him* [Peter], *what I am doing you do not understand now, but afterward you will understand.*" In other words, I'm going to do something, and it's about something else that foreshadows something to come.

The clue is in the response of Jesus to Peter's request for Him to wash his hands and head as well as his feet. "*Jesus said to him, the one who is bathed does not need to wash except for his feet, but is completely clean.*" So, clearly we're not talking about washing feet, we're talking about total cleanliness. *You are clean, but not every one of you.* Of course, referring to Judas. In other words, Jesus' act of cleansing, washing their feet, was pointing to a greater act of cleansing that He was about to do. In fact, that greater act was *what He had come to do*, and this example was getting them ready for it.

In just a few hours from this act, Jesus would not remove His outer garments, He would be stripped of all of His garments. He would not serve by getting on His knees, He would serve by getting on a cross. He would not pour water into a bowl, He would pour out His blood. If you think it's humiliating to wash feet, imagine dying for sins. Behold the heart of your King.

The gospel is on full display here in this passage. It is this: Jesus did not come to wash the dirt off your feet. Jesus came to wash away the sin from your life. This is pointing you to something greater, because your ultimate problem is not that your feet are dirty, it's that your heart is. You have been stained with sin, and what can wash away my sin? Nothing but the blood of Jesus. He came for a much greater act of cleansing than washing feet. Just a few short hours after this moment, he fulfilled it.

This is the passage that shows the love of Jesus in full display. His lowliness as He serves. This small but shocking act pointing us to the larger work that He had come to do on the cross. So, what do we learn from it? First of all, qualification for ministry, that is serving Jesus, does not require a Master's of Divinity, it's being a servant with humility. I'm all for theological education, but at the end of the day, that's not what makes us qualified for ministry.

What makes us qualified for ministry is our willingness to get low. Are we willing to serve? Otherwise, we'll end up like Judas. Judas spent three years listening to the best preacher ever. Judas was a part of the best small group you could ever be a part of. Judas was involved in the most incredible hands-on ministry you could possibly see, and he was disqualified. Why? Because he had information, but he never had transformation. The truth of the matter of is, you can know all of this and not be qualified for ministry.

Jesus is saying, "I want servants of humility that go out into the world and show the world my heart."

Secondly, there is a direct relationship between lowliness and love. That is, the lower you go, the more love you show, which is why I say to you that no one has loved you like Jesus, because no one has gone as low for you as Jesus. And in all of our relationships, we need to understand that if we're really going to love our kids, if we're really going to love a spouse, if we're really going to love our church, if we're really going to love those we work with, we've got to go low.

The lower you go, the more you love. By the way, going low doesn't mean that you go low grudgingly, hating it. The heart really matters here. You genuinely want to sacrifice yourself for the good of others.

Thirdly, true joy is found when you live that way. It's found in service, not status. Jesus actually says, " Blessed is the one who does this." Do you want a blessed life? Do you want a happy life? A joy-filled life? A grace-filled life? It comes through serving.

Many Christians are big smiles and sad eyes. If you are one of them it is because you have missed this. The heart isn't happy because the heart is consumed with you.

The moment that you begin to let go and get rid of yourself and serve, you begin to experience true joy.

Fourthly, ongoing service to others is going to require ongoing repentance with God. You say, "Where are you getting this?" I'm taking this from the exchange between Jesus and Peter. "You are clean, but I must wash your feet."

When you put your faith in Jesus, you are completely clean before God. There is no condemnation for those who are in Christ Jesus. And yet the Bible, in multiple places, commands us to confess our sin before God. That is, we are clean in our being, and yet we keep getting dirty in our behavior. Therefore, we must continually come to God and confess our sins. I would go so far as to say that we're not ready for service until we've gone through repentance.

When you've repented, you're ready to serve because there is a direct relationship between going low with God, and then the ability to go low with others. The very thing that's keeping you from repentance is pride, which is the very thing keeping you from serving your brother or sister. If you're not willing to go low in repentance, you'll never go low in service. So, you are clean. Confess your dirt. Let Him wash your feet. And then you'll be ready to be used by God.

Lastly, you will never be clean without Christ. It's so clear in the passage, physical baths can't clean sinful souls. You must be willing to get low by confessing your sin and putting your faith in Jesus Christ. Of all of those reading this book, some of you are clean, but not all of you are. Who is the reader who is not clean? If you would be willing to get low and confess your sins, and believe in Jesus, He will say to you what He said to Peter, "You are clean." Only Jesus can do that in your life.

You've heard the name of Winston Churchill. He had a butler that took care of him, even helped him get dressed in the morning. Churchill always treated him like dirt. One particular morning, Churchill was rude to his butler, and his butler uncharacteristically got rude back. Churchill got upset at this and pouted for the rest of the day. Later in the day, Churchill said to his butler, "You were very rude to me this morning." The butler said, "Well, you were very rude to me." Churchill said, "Yes, but I am a great man."

Isn't that how we tend to think about it? That the greater you are, the more you ought to be served. To that, I say, behold the heart of your King. See the side of your Savior dripping with sacrificial humility. Gaze upon the One who loves you so much, He went low, even to the point of death on the cross. As you see that side of the Savior, don't forget Paul's words to the Philippians. "*Let this mind be in you which was also in Christ Jesus....*" In other words, Christian, as you go out into the world, make sure you take the heart of your King with you.

ABOUT THE AUTHOR

Dr. Wesley L. Feltner has spent the last 23 years serving local churches in the areas of preaching, leadership, missions, discipleship, and family ministries. He holds a BA in Organizational Communication, a M.Div. in Theology and Ph.D. in Leadership. He is a pastor, professor, missionary, and leader.

Born in Tennessee to faithful Christian parents, Dr. Feltner has served churches in Kentucky, North Carolina, Indiana, and Illinois and Minnesota. He and his family currently reside in the South Metro of the Twin Cities. He enjoys sports, fishing, reading, and a bold cup of coffee.

Most of all, he finds his greatest joy is seeing lives transformed by the power of the Gospel.

Made in the USA
Columbia, SC
27 December 2019